EMPLOYMENT TRIBUNAL CLAIMS

Tony Brown, Helen Mortlock, Claire Rankin

and

Annelise Tracy Phillips

London: The Stationery Office

Applications for reproduction should be made in writing to The Stationery Office Limited, St Crispins, Duke Street, Norwich NR3 1PD.

The information contained in this publication is believed to be correct at the time of manufacture. Whilst care has been taken to ensure that the information is accurate, the publishers can accept no responsibility for any errors or omissions or for changes to the details given.

A CIP catalogue for this book is available from the British Library.
A Library of Congress CIP catalogue record has been applied for.

First published 2000.

ISBN 0 11 702393 0

Printed in the United Kingdom by The Stationery Office
TJ2263   C0   9/00   19585   542795

Published by The Stationery Office and available from:

The Stationery Office
(mail, telephone and fax orders only)
PO Box 29, Norwich NR3 1GN
General enquiries/Telephone orders 0870 600 5522
Fax orders 0870 600 5533
www.the-stationery-office.co.uk

The Stationery Office Bookshops
123 Kingsway, London WC2B 6PQ
020 7242 6393 Fax 020 7242 6412
68–69 Bull Street, Birmingham B4 6AD
0121 236 9696 Fax 0121 236 9699
33 Wine Street, Bristol BS1 2BQ
0117 926 4306 Fax 0117 929 4515
9–21 Princess Street, Manchester M60 8AS
0161 834 7201 Fax 0161 833 0634
16 Arthur Street, Belfast BT1 4GD
028 9023 8451 Fax 028 9023 5401
The Stationery Office Oriel Bookshop
18–19, High Street, Cardiff CF1 2BZ
029 2039 5548 Fax 029 2038 4347
71 Lothian Road, Edinburgh EH3 9AZ
0870 606 5566 Fax 0870 606 5588

The Stationery Office's Accredited Agents
(see Yellow Pages)
and through good booksellers

CONTENTS

CHAPTER 1

Overview of claims in the Employment Tribunals

What is a Tribunal?

Employment Tribunals are the forum in which most legal disputes between employer and employee are resolved. They are intended to provide the parties with a quick, informal and efficient method of resolving their legal differences. Only the employee can bring proceedings in the Employment Tribunal (ET) but in some circumstances the employer can counter-claim once a case has been started by the employee.

Parties do not need legal representation in the ET, they can present their cases themselves. There is no legal aid for cases in the ET but employees in particular will be able to get advice and assistance from a number of sources, in particular the Citizens' Advice Bureau (CAB), law centres and the Free Representation Unit (FRU). Many law firms now also take on employment cases on a no-win no-fee basis. This means that the employee who brings the case does not need to pay the lawyer up front but if they win, they will share a specified proportion of their award of damages with the firm.

The style of the ET is informal and communications with it in most cases do not need to be in any special form. For most matters a simple letter setting out what the party is asking for will be sufficient.

The Clerk

Each case is assigned a clerk who will deal with the administrative matters such as listing and dealing with the attendance of the parties. Any queries in relation to administrative matters should be addressed to the clerk.

The Parties

Cases are brought by the employee (or ex-employee) who will fill out a form called an Originating Application (form IT1). Once a case has been started the employee will be called the Applicant. For details on how the form is filled out and what to do with it, see chapter 2. The employer will then be sent a Notice of Originating Application by the ET (form IT2) and a blank Notice of Appearance (form IT3) to fill out. Once the IT3 is registered the employer will then be referred to as the Respondent. For details of how to fill out the IT3, see chapter 3. Chapter 4 deals with how to amend either form and to add new parties.

The Tribunal

The decision-making body, called the Tribunal, is made up of three members drawn from 3 panels:

- of legally qualified persons with seven years', or more, experience
- of employer groups
- of employee groups.

Each member of the Tribunal has an equal vote and all can participate equally in the running of the case, although the Chairperson (the legally qualified member sitting in the middle) will normally direct the proceedings. The ET is designed so that its decisions are based on knowledge of the law and good industrial practice. It can decide unanimously or by a majority vote so that the Chairperson can be outvoted by the lay-members. This does not affect the validity of the decision and is not grounds for appeal.

Chairperson sitting alone

In some cases the Chairperson can sit alone, but before doing so he/she must consider the following matters:

- the wishes of the parties
- whether a dispute over the facts of what happened is likely, making it desirable that the case should be heard by a full Tribunal
- whether there is likely to be a dispute on the law which is better heard by the Chairperson sitting alone.

Cases in which a Chairperson normally sits alone include:

- where the parties give their written consent
- claims of unlawful deductions from wages
- applications for interim relief in trade union and health and safety cases
- breach of contract claims
- where either of the parties has indicated that they do not intend to contest the proceedings.

A full list of the cases a Chairperson may consider alone is featured in Appendix 1.

Common claims brought in the ET

This section only gives the briefest overview of some of the more common claims brought in the ET. For a full list, see Appendix 2.

Unfair dismissal

This is the most common type of claim brought in the ET. Most employees with more than one year's continuous employment with the same employer or with an associated employer have the right not to be unfairly dismissed. There are some exceptions. There are only five fair reasons why an employee can be dismissed:

- *Redundancy* – that is where there is a reduction or cessation of the employers' need for workers of a particular kind to do work, or to do work in a particular place. Redundancy also occurs where the employer has an expectation that either of these things will occur. A fair selection process and proper consultation need to be followed.

- *Conduct* – where the conduct of the employee is such that the employer is justified in dismissing them. Failure to obey reasonable orders, dishonesty, fighting, harassment or breaches of work rules can all be acts of misconduct. Some serious misconduct will justify immediate (summary) termination but normally a process of warnings for more minor acts will be followed.

- *Capability* – where the employee is incapable of doing the job. This will include incapability on grounds of ill health or poor performance. It may even include the lack of the proper skills and qualifications.

- *Some other substantial reason of a kind justifying dismissal* – or SOSR as it is usually known. This encompasses reasons which do not fall within the other categories but are still sufficient to justify dismissal.

- *Statutory bar* – where there is a statutory bar on the individual being employed to do that role.

In addition to showing that there was a fair reason for dismissal, the employer also has to show that the decision to dismiss for that reason was fair in all the circumstances. This means that the employer will have to show that a fair procedure was followed (this includes redundancy cases) and that the penalty imposed was reasonable.

Some reasons for dismissal will be automatically unfair even if a fair procedure was followed:

- Health and safety related dismissals

- Union related dismissals

- Maternity related dismissals (including the refusal of the right to return to work after maternity leave)

- Dismissal of employee representatives carrying out their duties

- Dismissal of shop workers who refuse Sunday working

- Working time related dismissals (e.g., refusal to exclude the limit on maximum working hours) (see below)

- Minimum wage dismissals

- Public interest disclosure dismissals

- Dismissals on a transfer of an undertaking unless there is an economic, technical or organisational reason justifying dismissal

- Dismissal for a spent conviction

- Dismissals relating to the duties of a pension trustee

- Selection for redundancy on the above grounds

- Dismissal for asserting a statutory right (provided the belief in the right is genuine, no right need actually exist)

- Dismissals for taking parental or family emergency leave (see below).

Dismissal includes the expiry of a fixed term contract, dismissal with or without notice and constructive dismissal. Constructive dismissal happens where the employer either in one incident or in a series of incidents behaves in such a way as to fundamentally breach the contract of employment and therefore entitles the employee to resign as a response. This type of dismissal normally occurs where the employer has tried to change the employee's employment terms in some fundamental way, but has not obtained the consent of the employee, or where the behaviour of the employer is such that it fundamentally undermines his/her duty to maintain the relationship of trust and confidence which ought to exist between the parties to the employment relationship.

Where the Applicant is claiming that he/she has been constructively dismissed, the burden of proving the dismissal is on him/her. The standard of proof is not that found in criminal cases, i.e., beyond reasonable doubt, but the normal civil standard, i.e., on the balance of probabilities (it is more likely than not that there has been a fundamental breach of the contract which goes to the root of it and indicates that the party who committed it no longer intends to be bound by the contract).

If the dismissal has been admitted by the Respondent, then the Respondent has the burden of proof to show that the dismissal was fair.

Whichever of the parties has the burden of proof tends to go first in the ET hearing (see chapter 8).

If a claim is successful, the Applicant can get an order for:

- *Reinstatement* – this means that the Applicant goes back to their job on the same terms and conditions receiving full back pay for the time out of work. Any earnings or social security payments are set off.

- *Re-engagement* – this means that the Applicant goes back to work for the same employer but in a different job with full back pay.

- *Compensation* – this is made up of a basic award which is calculated in the same way as a redundancy payment (see below) and a compensatory award which seeks to compensate for the losses the Applicant has suffered attributable to the actions of the Respondent. This is subject to a maximum payment of £50,000.

Reinstatement and re-engagement are rare; by far the most usual remedy is compensation.

Claims for unfair dismissal must be brought within three months from the date of dismissal unless it was not reasonably practicable to do so, in which case the claim must be brought within such further period as the ET considers reasonable.

For a list of time limits for all claims, see Appendix 3.

Sex and race discrimination

Claims of sex and race discrimination in connection with employment are also brought in the ET. Discrimination in these cases is prohibited by the Sex Discrimination Act 1975 and the Race Relations Act 1976. Race for these purposes includes colour, race, nationality, or ethnic or national origins. It does not include religion unless this is linked with ethnic origin. Claims can also be brought for discrimination on grounds of another's ethnic origin, for example, racist comments about others which may offend the employee.

Sex discrimination includes discrimination on ground of marital status and pregnancy or maternity.

Employees, job applicants, and contract workers can also claim discrimination. It is important to remember that employees can make claims and still remain in employment. They will then be protected by the rules against victimisation (see below). All areas of employment are covered:

- *Discriminatory advertising* – only the two commissions (Equal Opportunities Commission (EOC) and Commission for Racial Equality (CRE)) can bring claims in respect of this, but unsuccessful job applicants can use discriminatory adverts to raise a presumption that there has been discrimination in the selection process.

- *Engagement,* including selection and the terms of engagement.

- *Opportunities for promotion, transfer or training,* once the person is in role.

- *Dismissal for a discriminatory reason.*

- *Any other detriment* – for example, harassment.

Applicants can seek help and advice from the appropriate Commission which may also provide legal representation or funding.

There are various types of discrimination:

- *Direct discrimination* – this is where a person is treated less favourably than another person is, or would have been, on grounds of their sex or race, i.e., but for their race, sex or marital status, the person would have been treated the same.

- *Indirect discrimination* – this is where, on the face of it, a non-discriminatory, universal requirement is imposed but the proportion of women, or a particular ethnic or racial group, which can comply with the requirement is considerably smaller than the proportion of men, or the dominant ethnic or racial group, which can comply. The condition has to operate so as to disadvantage the Applicant and must not be justified. A condition will be justified if there is a reasonable balance between the discriminatory effect and the reasonable needs of the Respondent. A good example is the imposition of the requirement to perform a role full time. ETs have held that because more women than men bear the responsibility for childcare, the proportion of women who can comply with the obligation to work full time is considerably smaller. A requirement to perform a job full time must therefore be justified.

- *Harassment* – this is a type of direct discrimination in that it is a disadvantage to which a person is subjected on grounds of their race or sex. There is no statutory definition of harassment but ETs normally refer to the European Recommendation and Code of Practice on the Dignity of Women and Men at Work (91/131/EEC) which defines harassment as: 'unwanted conduct of a sexual nature or other conduct based on sex affecting the dignity of women and men at work. This can include unwelcome physical, verbal or non-verbal conduct' The CRE defines racial harassment as: 'unwanted conduct of a racial nature, or other conduct based on race, affecting the dignity of women and men at work'. It is important to remember that the test of whether behaviour is unwanted is subjective, i.e., looked at from the viewpoint from the person who alleges they have been harassed. In some cases where the behaviour complained about is particularly bad it will not be necessary for the person to have made it clear to the harasser that it is unwanted and for the behaviour to be repeated before a claim can be made. Further, a single act can amount to harassment if it is bad enough. There does not have to be a pattern of behaviour. In other, less obvious cases it will be necessary for the victim to have made the fact that the behaviour is unwanted clear and for there to be a repeat of the offending behaviour before the actions will amount to harassment. Employers are liable for the acts of their employees and agents unless they can show that they have taken all such steps as are reasonably practicable to prevent the act or acts of that nature from taking place. This will include having a special harassment complaints procedure in place and ensuring that it is widely known about, ensuring managers are trained and dealing with internal complaints effectively. The person who has allegedly committed the act of harassment can be named as a Respondent as well as the employer and the ET can make a specific award of damages against him/her.

- *Victimisation* – this is where the applicant is treated less favourably because they have threatened to bring proceedings, given evidence or information, taken any action or made any allegation by reference to the discrimination acts or actually doing any of those things. Allegations which are not made in good faith are not protected acts.

Some types of discrimination are allowed:

- positive discrimination in favour of women or men in relation to training if in the previous 12 months there was no one, or comparatively few, of that sex doing the job at that employer

- positive discrimination in favour of persons of a particular racial group where there are no persons of that group doing the job at that site

- positive discrimination in favour of persons of a particular racial group where the proportion of the persons of that group doing the job is small in comparison to the proportion of persons of that group who work at that employer or in relation to the catchment area from which he/she draws his/her recruits.

In some cases jobs can be restricted to certain racial groups:

- where the employee is to work wholly outside of the EU

- where the employment is in a private household

- dramatic performances or other entertainment where the person is chosen for authenticity

- as an artist's model or photomodel where authenticity is required

- where food or drink is to be served and a particular attribute is required for authenticity

- where personal services promoting a person's welfare are to be provided and these can most effectively be provided by a person of that racial group.

And to a specific gender (note – the same provisions apply to positive discrimination in favour of men):

- where the job requires a man for reasons of physiognomy (this does not include strength or stamina) or in dramatic performances for authenticity

- to preserve decency or privacy where the job involves physical contact with men or where they are undressed or using sanitary facilities and where they might reasonably object

- where the employee is to live in a private home and objection might reasonably be taken to a woman because of the degree of physical or social contact likely or the knowledge of the intimate details of a person's private life

- where it is impracticable for the employee to live elsewhere than the premises provided by the employer and the only available premises are not equipped with separate sleeping and sanitary facilities and it is not reasonable to expect the employer to provide them

- where the job is to be carried out in a prison, hospital or other special care establishment and all the persons there are men and given the essential nature of the establishment the job should not be held by a woman

- where personal services promoting a person's welfare are to be provided and these can most effectively be provided by a man

- where the job is one of two to be held by a married couple.

These exceptions should be treated with caution as they are interpreted narrowly by the ETs and if the employer already has enough persons of the relevant sex or racial group to carry out the service which is specified to be exceptional, the exclusions will no longer apply.

The burden of proving discrimination is on the Applicant. This can be discharged by demonstrating that there has been less favourable treatment. The Respondent must then show a non-discriminatory reason for the treatment. If he/she cannot, the ET is entitled (but not required) to draw an inference of discrimination.

Claims must be brought within three months of the act complained of. The time limit can be extended if the ET believes this to be just and equitable.

If a claim of discrimination is successful then the ET may make:

- an order declaring the rights of the Applicant

- a recommendation that the Respondent take specified steps to reduce the adverse impact on the Applicant of the matters to which the complaint relates

- an award of compensation made up of an element for injury to feelings, damages for pain and suffering in relation to any personal injury suffered and compensation for any past and future financial loss suffered as a result.

There is no maximum award.

Unlawful deductions from wages

Except to recover overpayments of wages, an employer is not allowed to make any deductions from the wages earned by an employee and which are properly payable to him/her unless this is required or permitted by statute or the employee has previously agreed to the deduction. The agreement must be given prior to the event giving rise to the deduction. For example, if an employee owes the employer money and then agrees to pay this back out of wages, then this will be an unlawful deduction unless the agreement to deduct was given before the event which led to the employee owing the employer money.

Wages will include bonuses, statutory sick pay, statutory maternity pay, holiday pay and commission.

If the Applicant's claim is successful then he/she will be entitled to repayment of the deducted amount; and even if he/she does actually owe the employer money, the employer will not be able to recover an amount equivalent to the unlawfully deducted amount.

There are special rules for people who work in the retail trade which mean that, broadly speaking, an employer cannot deduct more than 10% of the employee's salary (with the exception of the final wage packet) in respect of stock or cash deficiencies and he/she must follow a special notification procedure.

The burden of proof is on the Applicant and claims must be brought within three months beginning with the date of the deduction, or within such further period as the Tribunal considers reasonable if it was not reasonably practicable to present the claim in time. Where a series of deductions occurs, the time limit starts with the last deduction.

Redundancy

Most employees with more than two years' continuous service with the same employer or an associated company are entitled to a payment if they are made redundant. Redundancy occurs where the employee is dismissed because his/her employer has ceased, or intends to cease, carrying on the business for the purpose of which the employee was employed, or to carry on that business in the place where he/she was employed. Redundancy also occurs where there is a reduction or cessation of the requirement of the business for employees to carry out work of a particular kind, or to carry out that work in the place where the employee was employed.

Where other work is available for the employee to do, he/she must be offered that work. If the work is wholly or partly different from the work the employee used to do then he/she has a four-week trial period in which to decide to accept the role. If he/she does not then he/she remains entitled to his/her redundancy payment. If the work is on the same terms and is a suitable alternative, then the employee must normally accept the role or he/she may lose the right to his/her payment. Conversely, if the employee is not offered the available alternative work, then the dismissal may be procedurally unfair (see above) and the employee may claim unfair dismissal. A redundancy payment is based on a multiplier which depends on age and length of service. The multiplier is 1.5 weeks' pay for every year worked over the age of 41, 1 week's pay for every year worked over the age of 22 and 0.5 week's pay for each year worked over 18. A week's pay is capped at £230.

There are special rules which relate to redundancies of more than 20 employees within 90 days and which require the employer to consult with elected representatives or trade union representatives. If the employer does not do so, then the employee can make a complaint to the ET which can make an award of up to 30 days' pay where 30 days' consultation should have been given, and 90 days' pay where 90 days' consultation should have been given. Note that for these purposes pay is not limited to a particular amount.

In the case of a dismissal of 20 or more employees within a 90-day period the employer must consult for 30 days; and 90 days where 100 or more are to be dismissed.

There is a statutory presumption that dismissed employees have the right to a redundancy payment so the burden of proving they do not is on the Respondent. Claims must be made within six months starting with the date of dismissal. The Tribunal has the right to extend the time limit for a further six months where this is just and equitable.

Disability discrimination

Where a person is disabled for the purposes of the Disability Discrimination Act 1995 particular rules apply. A person is disabled for these purposes if he/she has a physical or mental impairment which has a substantial and long-term effect on his/her ability to carry out normal day-to-day activities.

These are:

- mobility

- manual dexterity

- physical co-ordination

- continence

- the ability to lift, carry or otherwise move everyday objects

- speech, hearing or eyesight

- memory or ability to learn, concentrate or understand

- perception of the risk of physical danger.

Long-term effects are those which last, are expected to last or to recur over a 12-month period or to last for the lifetime of the employee. There are special rules which exclude addiction to alcohol or non-medically prescribed drugs and include facial disfigurements in the definition. Conditions which at first do not have a substantial effect but which will increase in severity such as cancer or AIDS are deemed to be disabilities as soon as there is any effect on the activities set out above. Discrimination on grounds of past disability is also covered.

There are guidance notes that can be obtained from the Department for Education and Employment which will help in determining which conditions amount to a disability.

If a person is disabled for these purposes, then he/she has the right not to be discriminated against on grounds of his/her disability unless this is justified. The areas covered are the same as those set out above in relation to sex and race discrimination. Employers are also under an obligation to make reasonable adjustments to working arrangements and physical features which place the employee at a substantial disadvantage. The reasonableness of the adjustment is measured according to:

- the extent to which taking the step would prevent the effect in question

- the extent to which it is practicable for the employer to take the step

- the financial and other costs which would be incurred by the employer in taking the step and the extent to which taking it would disrupt any of his/her activities

- the extent of the employer's financial and other resources

- the availability to the employer of financial or other assistance with respect to taking the step.

The guidance notes refer to some ways in which reasonable adjustments can be made, for example, duties can be changed as can hours of work, equipment can be modified or purchased, premises can be adjusted and time off work can be given.

Unlawful discrimination can therefore occur in a number of ways:

- *A failure to make a reasonable adjustment which is not justified.* A failure to make an adjustment will be justified if the reason for the failure is material to the circumstances of the particular case (i.e., in relation to that employee and not to the disabled population in general) and substantial.

- *Direct discrimination (see above) on grounds of disability which is not justified.* Direct discrimination can be justified if the reason for it is both material to the circumstances of the particular case and substantial. This is a low threshold and the reason only needs to be something more than minor or trivial. Note: where the employer has failed to make a reasonable adjustment, direct discrimination cannot be justified unless it would have been justified had the adjustment been made.

- *Harassment* – see above.

- *Victimisation* – see above.

Again, claims of disability discrimination are not restricted to employees and there is no requirement to have 1 year's service before a claim can be made. (See above – race and sex discrimination.) The burden of proof is on the Applicant and the time limit is the same as in other discrimination complaints. Again, if an Applicant is successful the ET can award the same remedies as in sex and race discrimination cases.

Working Time Regulations

These Regulations apply to 'workers', including casual and contract workers, and give rights to:

- a maximum working week of 48 hours averaged over a 17-week period unless the worker signs an individual opt out

- a rest break of 20 minutes where the working day lasts for 6 hours or more

- a daily rest break of 11 hours in 24

- a weekly rest break of either one uninterrupted period of 48 hours in 14 days or two uninterrupted periods of 24 hours in 14 days

- a restriction on night working of an average of 8 hours in 24 over a 17-week averaging period

- free health assessments for night workers

- 4 weeks' holiday a year (Bank Holidays are included).

There are special rules for managers who control their own hours of work, young people and some industries are exempted. In addition, many of the rights can be altered or reduced if there is an agreement with the recognised trade union or if a workforce agreement with employee representatives has been reached.

Workers have the right not to be subjected to any detriment:

- because they have either refused or proposed to refuse to comply with a requirement which the employer intends to impose or imposes in breach of the Regulation

- because they have failed to sign a workforce agreement to vary the Regulations

- because they have refused to forgo a right to which they are entitled under the Regulations

- because they are a workforce representative and have performed their functions

- because they have brought proceedings against their employer to enforce a right

- because they have alleged that their employer has infringed a right.

If they are successful, workers can claim an amount which is just and equitable taking into account the loss suffered. There is no maximum award. Claims must be brought within three months of the date of the act complained of, or within such further time as is reasonable if it is not reasonably practicable to present the claim in time.

Where the employer prevents the worker taking advantage of rest breaks, the ET can again award a just and equitable amount taking into account the employer's default and the losses sustained by the worker.

Employees who are dismissed because:

- they have refused to comply with an instruction which is in contravention of the Regulations

- they refuse to forego a right under the Regulations

- they have failed to sign up to a workforce agreement to vary the Regulations

- they are a workforce representative, propose to become one and have carried a function or proposed to, as a representative

are automatically unfairly dismissed (see above). For dismissals related to activities as a representative, a minimum award of £2,900 is in place.

Time off

Employees are entitled to time off in certain circumstance:

- trade union officials are entitled to time off to carry out official duties and to undergo approved and relevant training (paid)

- trade union members are entitled to time off to take part in certain trade union activities (unpaid)

- all employees are entitled to time off to carry out public duties such as acting as a Justice of the Peace or ET member (unpaid)

- employees under threat of redundancy and who have been given notice of dismissal have the right to reasonable time off to look for new work or to make arrangements for training for new employment (paid)

- pregnant women are entitled to time off for antenatal care (paid)

- employee representatives are entitled to time off to perform their functions and participate in elections (paid)

- safety representatives are entitled to time off to perform their duties and to undergo training (paid)

- trustees of pension funds (paid).

If the time off is refused then the employee has the right to make a claim in the ET. Where the entitlement is to paid time off, in the main the remedy will be for the pay; if it is for unpaid leave, the ET will award a figure which is just and equitable in all the circumstances.

The Transfer of Undertakings (Protection of Employment) Regulations 1981 (as amended) ('TUPE')

TUPE applies whenever there is a transfer of an undertaking or a business (or part) from one employer to another. An undertaking is capable of being transferred if it is a stable economic entity – an organised grouping of persons and assets – whose activity is not limited to performing one specific works contract or mere administrative functions. The essential question is – does the entity retain its identity after the transfer?

Employees who are employed in the undertaking to be transferred immediately prior to the transfer have the right to transfer with the undertaking. Employees may object to the transfer to the new employer by informing either the old employer or the new employer they object to becoming employed by the new employer. If an employee does object, then the transfer operates so as to terminate the employee's contract of employment but the employee is not treated as having been dismissed and therefore has no right to claim unfair dismissal.

However, if the employee's objection stems from his/her knowledge that he/she will subjected by the new employer to changes in his/her working conditions which are substantial and to his/her detriment he/she will have the right to refuse to transfer and claim constructive dismissal against the new employer.

Broadly speaking, TUPE means that the contract of the employment of any employees who transfer is deemed to operate after the transfer as if it always existed between the employee and the new employer. This has the following consequences:

- the new employer is obliged to honour the existing terms and conditions of the transferring employees with the exception of pension entitlement

- continuous employment transfers

- liabilities arising in connection with the employment relationship transfer

- recognition and any collective agreements transfer

- liability for any course of action taken by the employer, e.g., disciplinary action transfers

- if the employee is dismissed by reason of the transfer then the dismissal will be automatically unfair unless there is an economical, technical or organisational reason entailing a change in the numbers or functions of the workforce

- a change in terms and conditions at any time will be ineffective if the reason for it is the transfer.

- where employees are transferred from one employer to another under TUPE, both the old and the new employer have duties to inform, and potentially to consult with, the appropriate representatives which may include representatives of a recognised trade union in relation to any employees who may be affected by the transfer or by measures taken in relation to it. There are special rules about how and when information and consultation must take place, but if there is a failure to inform and consult then each affected employee can bring a claim in the Employment Tribunal for up to 13 weeks' pay unless the employer can show that there were special circumstances justifying their failure. Claims must be brought within three months but where this is not reasonably practicable, the ET has a discretion to extend for such further period as is reasonable.

Equal pay

The Equal Pay Act 1970 implies into every person's contract of employment an equality clause. Although the Equal Pay Act applies to both men and women, normally employees disadvantaged in this area are women. Where a woman can show that she is in the same employment as a man who is engaged on:

- like work (the same or broadly similar work)

- work which is equivalent and has been rated as equivalent under a job evaluation scheme

- work is of equal value

she has the right to have any less favourable terms in her contract modified so as to make it not less favourable, or to have implied into her contract any more favourable terms.

Men and women are in the same employment for these purposes if they are employed by the same employer or an associated employer:

- at the same establishment

- at different establishments where common terms and conditions of employment apply either generally or for the relevant employees.

Unless the employer can demonstrate that there is a genuine material factor which explains the difference in pay, and which is not due to a difference in sex, the employee can make a claim in the ET for the loss to pay for up to six years before the proceedings have started.

There is no limit on the amount of back pay which can be awarded.

The burden of proof is on the Applicant unless the pay system used lacks transparency; if this is the case, the burden may shift to the employer to show no discrimination in pay has occurred. Claims must be brought within six months of the last date of employment.

The following genuine material factors have been held to justify a difference in pay:

- scarcity of suitably qualified employees to fill the post

- late night working

- mistake.

Note that if the genuine material factor itself is indirectly discriminatory, then it will need to be objectively justified in order to provide a proper defence to the complaint. That means that if the justification for the difference in pay affects a greater proportion of women than men, it must be objectively justified itself in that it must correspond to a real need of the employer and be proportionate to satisfy that need.

There are extremely complicated rules in relation to equal pay claims in the ET. For a discussion of some of those rules, see chapter 10.

Breach of contract claims

Where the employee's contract of employment has been breached by the employer, the claim arises, or is outstanding, at the termination of the employee's employment and is connected with the employment (other than personal injury claims), the employee can bring that claim in the ET provided it does not relate to:

- terms requiring the employer to provide living accommodation for the employee

- terms imposing obligations on the employer or the employee in connection with living accommodation

- terms in restraint of trade

- terms in relation to obligation of confidence

- terms relating to intellectual property.

Normally employees will bring claims for breach of contract in the ET where the employer has breached the contract of employment by not giving the employee the appropriate contractual or statutory notice. In this respect it is important to remember that the employer is not required to give notice of termination where the employee has committed a fundamental breach of the contract of employer which entitles the employer to dismiss summarily, i.e., without notice.

If, however, the contract has been breached, then a claim can be made in the ET for up to £25,000. Claims above this amount should be raised in the High Court or County Court.

In some cases, if employees are dismissed without notice shortly before they accrue sufficient continuity of service to claim unfair dismissal and there is no provision in the contract allowing the employer to terminate immediately upon payment in lieu of notice, the employees may be able to claim compensation for the loss of the chance to claim unfair dismissal. This means that the Tribunal has to assess what the prospects are of an unfair dismissal claim succeeding had the employee been allowed to bring it, and will compensate the employee accordingly as part of the breach of contract complaint.

Employers can counter-claim for any monies which the employee owes them provided the employer does this within six weeks of receiving the IT1.

The burden of proof is on the party asserting the breach and claims must be brought within three months of the date of termination of employment unless this is not reasonably practicable, in which case the ET can extend the time limit by such time as is reasonable.

Parental leave

Employees with more than one year's continuous service have the right to take parental leave in respect of children born on or after 15 December 1999 and who are under five years old or adopted children under the age of eighteen. There are special rules for children with disabilities.

In broad terms employees can take a maximum of 13 weeks' leave within the 5-year period. If the employer and employees have not implemented a special parental leave policy, then the government fall-back scheme applies which provides that:

- leave can only be taken in blocks or multiples of one week

- employees have to give a minimum notice of 21 days

- a maximum of four weeks' leave per year can be taken

- the employer may postpone leave for up to six months where business is unduly disrupted unless the leave is to be taken immediately after the child is born.

There is also a right to take reasonable time off for family emergencies during working hours in order to:

- make arrangements for the provision of care for a dependant who is ill or injured

- provide assistance on an occasion where a dependant falls ill, gives birth or is injured or assaulted

- in consequence of the death of the dependant

- because of the unexpected disruption or termination of arrangements of the care of a dependant

- deal with an incident which involves a child and occurs during a period when an educational establishment is responsible for him or her.

Dependants are wives, husbands, children, parents or others who live in the same household but are not lodgers.

The right to both types of time off is unpaid but employees are protected against being dismissed because they have taken parental leave or time off to care for dependants. In such cases any dismissal is automatically unfair (see above) and subjecting an employee to a detriment as a consequence of the above will mean that the employee can make a claim in the ET for compensation which is just and equitable having regard to the default of the employer (see similar claims under the Working Time Regulations, above).

Miscellaneous rights

There are various other claims which can be brought in the ET:

- claim for a guarantee payment where the employee is laid off

- the right not to suffer action short of dismissal for trade union activities or membership

- a right not to suffer action short of dismissal to compel union membership, whether in or outside a closed shop

- a right not to suffer action short of dismissal to compel payments in lieu of union membership

- a right not to be unlawfully excluded or expelled from the union in a closed shop

- a right not to be unjustifiably disciplined by a trade union

- a right not to be refused employment on grounds related to trade union membership

- a right not to be refused the service of an employment agency on grounds related to trade union membership

- a right not to suffer unauthorised deductions of union subscriptions

- the right to receive written statement of reasons for dismissal

- a right to receive a written statement of the particulars of employment or any alterations.

CHAPTER 2

How to start a claim

How claims are started

An employee bringing a claim in the ET must fill out an IT1 which can be obtained from the Employment Tribunal, Job Centre or Citizens' Advice Bureau (see Appendix 4). The form is relatively straightforward to fill out but claims can be started in the Tribunal by letter or on a home-made form provided it contains the following details:

- the Applicant's name and address or where he/she can be contacted in the UK

- the name and address of the Respondent

- the reasons, with particulars, for the complaint

Care should be taken when filling out the IT1 although the ET will allow a great deal of latitude to the unrepresented Applicant.

Box 1 of the IT1 asks the Applicant to set out the type of complaint he/she is making. If more than one complaint is being made, then all should be listed. The form should include details of the Applicant and any representative as well as the name of the person against whom the relief is sought. This will normally be the company rather than a particular manager (for discrimination rules, see later – chapter 10).

The most complex section of the IT1 is section 11 which requires the Applicant to set out the details of the complaint.

It is not necessary to set out the full background to the events which occurred, but only the relevant factors the Applicant is relying on in support of their complaint. Where documents are referred to, the Applicant should ensure that these are available to be provided to the Respondent although it is not necessary to attach documents such as e.g., dismissal letters to the IT1. If not enough detail is given the ET will order 'further particulars', i.e., more detail to be given.

Where a series of events is relied upon, e.g., in harassment complaints, details of the dates and parties to the events should be given and quotes of words said if they are relevant. It is not necessary to quote any law at this stage nor is it necessary to quote an Act upon which the Applicant relies.

Time Limits

In the ET most complaints must be brought within three or six months of the date of the act complained. Time limits are applied strictly. A list of the time limits of various claims is set out in Appendix 3. There are a number of broad principles which apply.

- Some claims must be brought within a particular time limit and there is no discretion to extend.

- The ET can extend some time limits if it is satisfied that it was not reasonably practicable for the complaint to be brought in time. If so, the time limit will be extended for such period as is reasonable.

- Some time limits can be extended where it is just and equitable to do so.

When does time start to run?

- Where the time limit starts beginning with a particular date, this date is counted. Applicants must count forward three or six calendar months (as appropriate) and take off one day. For example, if the start date is 12 June 2000 then a three month limit expires on 11 September 2000.

Presenting the claim

Completed IT1s should be sent to the appropriate local ET addressed to the Secretary. Details of addresses are set out within the form.

IT1s can be posted, but note the IT1 must arrive before the expiry of the limit. Again, this can be faxed or hand-delivered. Whatever the method used, it is up to the Applicant to check the form has arrived before the time limit expires.

This should be done by telephone.

Extending time

In many cases claims must be brought within a certain time period unless this is not reasonably practicable, in which case the Tribunal will extend the time limit for such further period as it considers reasonable (see chapter 1 for details of the types of claims in this category).

This is a two-stage test in which the Tribunal will enquire first of all whether it was reasonably practicable to put the complaint in time and, if not, whether it was brought within such further period as is reasonable.

Reasonable practicability

Numerous reasons for delayed submission of IT1s have been heard by the Tribunals. In summary, it is for the employee to prove that for some reason which was out of his/her hands, a delay occurred and that as soon as that reason ceased to take effect, the IT1 was submitted. Below are some reasons for delay adjudicated on by the Tribunal but it should be remembered that each case must be judged on its own facts and merits.

- *Wrong advice from advisors.* Case law indicates that where advisors are skilled, e.g., lawyers, trade union representatives or Citizens' Advice Bureau personnel, having received the wrong advice from advisors will not mean that it was not reasonably practicable to present the claim in time. Such claims will therefore be dismissed. If the advice is from an unskilled advisor, e.g., at the Job Centre, then this will be an explanation which is likely to satisfy the Tribunal that it was not reasonably practicable to present the claim in time.

- *Awaiting the outcome of internal appeals procedures.* This will not render it reasonably impracticable to present the claim in time unless the employer specifically encourages the employee to delay *(Owen v. Crown House 1973 {ALL ER 618}).*

- *Awaiting the outcome of other proceedings.* Although it may seem sensible to delay Employment Tribunal proceedings where these are related to, e.g., proceedings for theft in criminal trials, this rationale will not persuade the Tribunal that it was not reasonably practicable to present the claim in time.

- *Too ill/incapable of submitting complaint.* Tribunals have held in cases where employees became too sick, whether physically or mentally, to either give solicitors instructions or to present the claim themselves that it was not reasonably practicable for them to have done so.

- *Not knowing you have a claim.* Being ignorant of the fact that a right to complain exists is likely to be a reason the Tribunal will accept provided it was reasonable to be ignorant. Given the widespread publicity in relation to the complaints available in the Employment Tribunal it is most unlikely that employees will now be able to demonstrate that it is reasonable for them to be ignorant of their rights. Where employees are ignorant of the facts which give rise to the complaint, i.e., without knowledge of those facts the Applicant would not know that he/she has any complaint, this will justify a delay provided the facts of which knowledge is obtained are crucial to the decision to bring the claim.

- *Lost in the post.* If the Applicant can prove the date of posting and that the form should have arrived in time, getting lost in the post will be an acceptable reason for delay. Most Tribunals tend to assume that first-class mail will arrive on the second working day after posting, and second-class mail on the fourth working day.

Was the complaint submitted within a reasonable time frame?

Even if the Applicant can show it was not reasonably practicable for a complaint to be brought in time, he/she will still have to demonstrate that once that reason ceased to have effect there was no unreasonable delay in the presentation of the complaint. Applicants would therefore do well to submit a complaint as soon as possible even if initially their claim appears to be out of time. It may be that the time limit can be extended but any further delay which cannot be explained will be fatal.

The just and equitable extension

In many cases, and in particular in discrimination complaints, the Tribunal simply has a discretion to extend time where it is just and equitable to do so (for details, see chapter 7). This discretion is very widely used so that, e.g., in relation to these complaints the wrong advice from advisors is likely to persuade the Tribunal to exercise its discretion.

Each case is considered on its own merits with the prejudice to the Respondent as a consequence of the delay considered, as opposed to the injustice to the Applicant if the claim is rejected.

CHAPTER 3

How to defend a claim

How do you know a claim has been made?

The claim

Confirmation that a claim has been lodged against you will arrive by post from the local Employment Tribunal office. This will usually be sent to the place the employee worked or works and site-based staff will need to be able to recognise the importance of such documents and send them to the right person (usually the Human Resources Manager) without delay. The person making the claim is known as the Applicant.

In the envelope from the Employment Tribunal you will receive:

- The Applicant's Originating Application (Form IT1) setting out the nature of the complaint.

- Form IT2: this includes the Employment Tribunal's instructions for entering your defence, which is known as the Notice of Appearance. The employer/person against whom the claim is made is known as the Respondent.

- A blank Form IT3, for you to record your Notice of Appearance.

- A helpful booklet explaining how the Employment Tribunal process works.

Reviewing the claim

Do not be tempted to put the documents to one side to deal with later; you have only 21 days from the date of receipt to return your Notice of Appearance to the Tribunal. Extensions are possible but should not be relied upon as a matter of course (see below).

On receipt of the above documents, you should check the following points:

- The date you received the Originating Application – make a record of it. This could become important if there have been postal delays and there is an issue over when the 21-day period came to an end.

- Check the date stamp in the top right-hand corner of the IT1, to see when the Employment Tribunal received it and also the date on the second page, when it was signed by the Applicant.

Most Employment Tribunal claims must be lodged with the Tribunal within three months of the date of dismissal, or the act complained of. If the claim is potentially out of time (see chapters 1 and 3), then you would wish to highlight this in your Notice of Appearance, requesting a preliminary hearing for the Tribunal to determine at the earliest possible stage whether it has jurisdiction to hear the Applicant's claim. For more detail of preliminary hearings, see chapter 6.

- The Applicant's details, including job, workplace, length of service and wage details. You will find these in boxes 2, 4, 6, 7 and 8 of the Originating Application. You may need to seek information from another part of the business and from particular managers to complete the Notice of Appearance.

- Check Box 3 in the bottom left-hand corner. Is the Applicant represented and if so by whom? This could be, for example, by a Trade Union, a local advice centre or by a solicitor. If a representative has been instructed, the Employment Tribunal will send information about the case to that representative rather than to the Applicant personally, and you, the Respondent, should do the same.

- Who has the claim been made against? It is important to consider whether the Applicant has made his or her claim against the right employer. Was the Applicant your employee at one stage, but was transferred to another under the *Transfer of Undertakings (Protection of Employment) Regulations 1981?* It is possible in such circumstances that the claim should be against the new employer, the 'transferee'. Even if the transfer is in dispute between you and the new employer, it is best to write to the Employment Tribunal when you return the Notice of Appearance, to request that the new employer also be joined into the proceedings as the Second Respondent. Joinder of parties is permitted by Rule 17 of the Employment Tribunal Rules of Procedure – see Appendix 6.

   If the claim if one of discrimination, it is possible that an individual employee has also been mentioned as a Respondent in his or her own right. If so, that individual will also receive the documents set out in the section above on 'The Claim', and will need to return a separate Notice of Appearance. He/she may well seek your assistance. Always seek advice on these claims. Compensation for well-founded discrimination claims is unlimited by law and the employer Respondent's and the individual Respondent's interests in defending the action may not always coincide. If this is the case, the individual should seek his or her own advice.

- The explanation of the Applicant's claim in Box 11. What claim is the Applicant making (see chapter 1 for a description of the appropriate claims) and also, what remedy is sought? Where the Applicant is making a complaint arising from dismissal, he or she is asked to indicate on the application form whether he/she is seeking reinstatement, re-engagement or compensation only (see Box 10). A preference noted here does not, however, prevent the Applicant from changing his or her mind later. Furthermore, as you will see in chapter 9, if an Applicant wins his or her claim, the Employment Tribunal may have a duty to consider whether reinstatement or re-engagement is practicable and should be ordered. If it is not ordered, the Employment Tribunal will award compensation.

Responding to the claim

The 21-day time limit

The Respondent has 21 days from receipt of the Originating Application in which to lodge the Notice of Appearance with the Employment Tribunal (Rule 3 of the Employment Tribunal Rules).

When counting the 21 days, the date of receipt of the claim is day one and weekends are included. If you were to receive a claim on 1 February 2000, therefore, the 21 days would expire on 21 February 2000. You should aim to lodge the Notice of Appearance by close of business, which in the case of the Employment Tribunal office should be regarded as 4.00 p.m. If you do send it in later that day, it is unlikely that it would be considered late.

If you propose to instruct a representative, for example, a solicitor, to conduct the case for you, send them all the information set out in the 'Claim' and 'what information do you need' (following) sections of this chapter, as soon as possible, to enable the time limit to be complied with.

Are you unable to comply with the time limit?

This may happen where the manager you need to talk to is on holiday or the form is sent to the site where the Applicant worked and you do not receive it as quickly as you should.

In these circumstances, send a fax to the Employment Tribunal without delay, explaining the difficulty of complying and asking for an extension of time of a further seven or fourteen days, as needed. The Employment Tribunal has a discretion to extend time under its Rules of Procedure (see Rules 3(1), 3(2) and 15). You may be granted the extension and you must lodge your Notice of Appearance within the new timescale.

The other possibility is that you will receive a letter telling you to send the Notice of Appearance to the Employment Tribunal as soon as possible and the Tribunal will, upon receipt, consider whether or not to validate your Notice of Appearance. The letter may also highlight the potential cost implications of entering a late Notice of Appearance.

The costs rules allow the Applicant to apply for a contribution towards his or her costs, if the Respondent's conduct of the litigation is, amongst other things, unreasonable. If your delay in entering the Notice of Appearance is inordinate, i.e., well outside the 21-day time limit and shortly before or even at the hearing, but you are nevertheless permitted by the Tribunal to enter it, the Applicant will have good grounds to apply for a costs award against you (see chapter 9).

Provided you enter your Notice of Appearance within a short time after the 21-day limit, and have a reasonable explanation for the delay, a costs award is most unlikely.

The other risk you face in such circumstances is the Employment Tribunal refusing to hear your defence altogether. Rule 3(2)(a) (see Appendix 6) provides that a Respondent who does not enter a Notice of Appearance within 21 days is not entitled to take any part in the proceedings except to apply for an extension of time. In deciding whether to validate a late Notice of Appearance, a Tribunal will consider the following:

- the explanation, or lack of it, for the delay

- the merits or possible merits of the Respondent's defence

- the possible prejudice to the Respondent if they went unheard

- the prejudice to the Applicant of any delay in the proceedings as a result of the extension being granted

- whether an award of costs could compensate for any prejudice to the Applicant

- any other relevant factors.

The Tribunal would then balance the above factors to see if the Notice of Appearance, and hence the Respondent's participation in the proceedings, should be allowed in the interests of justice. Upon balancing the above factors in the case of *Gormley (Marble Specialists) Ltd v. Johnson EAT 1110/98,* the Employment Appeal Tribunal decided that the Respondent should NOT be permitted to have an extension of time to enter its Notice of Appearance.

The safest approach in these circumstances is to enter a 'skeleton' Notice of Appearance, to buy time to answer the claim in more detail. For example, if the Applicant claims he/she was unfairly dismissed, you may simply be able to summarise the reason for the dismissal and contend that the decision to dismiss the Applicant for that reason was fair and reasonable.

For example:

> *We deny that the Applicant was unfairly dismissed.*
>
> *The Applicant was dismissed for a fair reason, namely [conduct/capability/redundancy/illegality/some other substantial reason]* within the meaning of Section 98 of the Employment Rights Act 1996.*
>
> *We acted reasonably in dismissing the Applicant for this reason in accordance with equity and the substantial merits of the case.*
>
> *We therefore believe that the Applicant's dismissal was fair.*
>
> *We will supply a more detailed response in due course.*

*Remember there are only five potentially fair reasons for dismissal, which are those mentioned above (see also chapter 1). If your reason does not easily fall within these, seek advice on whether the 'some other substantial reason' category will help. If you do not have a potentially fair reason, the employee's dismissal will be unfair. If your reason for dismissal was a protected reason, for example, you dismissed the employee on the ground of her pregnancy or maternity leave, because the employee made a protected disclosure (i.e., blew the whistle), or raised concerns on certain health or safety issues or took part in trade union activities, the claim will be automatically unfair and potentially attract especially high awards. Compensation for whistleblowers and for individuals dismissed for raising certain health and safety issues is uncapped by law.

A full list of protected reasons is provided in chapter 1.

The Notice of Appearance

Completing the form IT3.

The Notice of Appearance is a printed Form IT3 and much of the information you are required to include is self-explanatory. A specimen form is at Appendix 5.

Box 1 – the Respondent's name and address. Make sure you include the company's full name, not the trading name or division, and the correct address with postcode, together with the name of the individual within the company to whom you want correspondence to be sent.

Box 2 – is where you enter your representative's details, for example, a solicitor or other adviser. If you do not have a representative, but wish the documents to be sent to another nominated person at another company address, for example, Head Office, then enter the details here.

It is extremely important to give the Employment Tribunal detailed information of where and to whom to send communications about the Tribunal process, and you may wish to make the address private and confidential. Failure to do this may result in letters and documents being opened in the normal course of post and circulated widely within the company before it finds a home. Not only may this result in you having insufficient notice of deadlines and hearing dates, but it may also encourage gossip and disquiet, particularly where the allegations are of a sensitive nature.

Box 3 – Unless you are absolutely sure you do not wish to defend the Applicant's claim, always tick the 'yes' box. If you are in any doubt whatsoever, tick the 'yes' box and seek advice.

Box 4 – if you terminated the Applicant's employment, then tick 'yes', you did dismiss, and you should state the reason for the dismissal. Remember, it must be one of the five potentially fair reasons.

If the Applicant resigned and is claiming constructive dismissal, or is still in employment, then you obviously tick the 'no' box.

Box 5 and 6 – you will see that the Applicant has given wages and benefits and length of service information on his/her application form. You should check whether or not it is correct. If not, enter the correct details here.

Box 7 – is where you enter the grounds of your defence. In this box you should ideally summarise both the facts and circumstances you believe establish your defence, and your arguments. The core unfair dismissal arguments are highlighted in the 'skeleton' Notice of Appearance featured above.

The Tribunal may have only the Originating Application and your Notice of Appearance to read in detail before the hearing. It is therefore helpful to give an overview of the relevant issues.

Use a separate piece of paper if you need to. You should explain what your business is, the Applicant's position and the sequence of events which led to his/her dismissal or the act complained of. Be aware that the Applicant or his/her representative is likely to ask for Further and Better Particulars (i.e., further information/detail) of broad statements such as 'the Applicant was selected for redundancy on the basis of fair and objective criteria'. Also, take care not to refer to matters detailed in Box 7 if you are unsure of the facts or their accuracy.

If you do subsequently discover that information in your Notice of Appearance is incorrect, you can write to the Tribunal requesting that your document be amended. The letter should set out the exact amendment you are seeking.

What information do you need?

If you do not have first-hand knowledge of the case, then the first step is to collect together all the documentary evidence. The Applicant's personnel file may include all the relevant paperwork, depending on the nature of the claim. If not, then the papers you may need to get together are likely to include:

- contract of employment and up-to-date wage details

- policies and procedural handbook (to include, for example, the disciplinary or grievance procedures and sickness rules)

- appraisal documentation and management performance reports, (particularly relevant to capability issues)

- notes of any investigatory, grievance, disciplinary or appeal hearings

- all correspondence including e-mails (relating to any material investigatory, grievance, disciplinary or appeal hearings, or the act complained of by the employee)

- any correspondence concerning either the dismissal or the act complained of

- any previous warnings.

It is important to note your obligations in respect of documents, in particular to keep safe relevant documents, whether or not you believe they help your case (see chapter 4 for more details).

How do you find out more detail of the Applicant's claim?

The Originating Application may not give you very much detail of the Applicant's complaint. The bare statement 'I believe I have been unfairly dismissed', without more, gives the employer little to go on. What the employer needs to know is why the Applicant believes that, before he/she can respond effectively.

In these circumstances, you should either send in a skeleton Notice of Appearance within 21 days or at least request an extension of time, stating the reason for your request. You should then write to the Applicant, or his/her nominated representative as appropriate, sending a copy to the Tribunal, asking for further and better particulars of the Applicant's complaint. A letter will do, and in the above example you would say something along these lines:

> In your Originating Application you state 'I believe I have been unfairly dismissed'.
>
> Please explain in detail why you believe you were unfairly dismissed.
>
> Please respond within 14 days, failing which I shall write to the Employment Tribunal to request an Order requiring your compliance.

If the Applicant, or his/her representative, does not respond as requested, write to the Employment Tribunal at the end of the time limit set, enclosing a copy of your letter and explain that you have received no reply and would like an Order that the Applicant gives the further and better particulars required within a specified time.

Obtaining further and better particulars, and also other information to help you prepare your case, are explored in more detail in chapter 4.

Lodging the Notice of Appearance

Once you have completed the Form IT3, you must send it to the Employment Tribunal. The details of the Tribunal and the case reference number, which you should quote in all communications with the Employment Tribunal, will be found on the Form IT2.

Send the Notice of Appearance form plus a short covering letter by post or by fax. Often when you fax the form, the Employment Tribunal would prefer you not to post a hard copy in addition, in order to avoid duplication. Always use the fax if you are up against a time limit, and it is a good practice to telephone the Employment Tribunal once the fax has gone through, to check that it has been safely received and, if appropriate, to ask whether you should also send a hard copy.

The covering letter need do no more than confirm who you are, the fact you are instructed if you are the representative, and enclose the Notice of Appearance. If the Originating Application is sent to the Employment Tribunal late, then your letter should also request a preliminary hearing to determine whether or not the Employment Tribunal has jurisdiction to hear the Applicant's claim (see Chapter 6).

Upon receipt of the Notice of Appearance, the Tribunal office will copy it to the Applicant (or his/her representative) and its next major step is to set a hearing date. The speed with which matters come to hearing varies between tribunals regionally. Generally speaking you should work on the basis that a hearing may take place at any time from six weeks after the Notice of Appearance is lodged, so try not to leave everything to the last minute. If the Respondent's witnesses are not available for some weeks within the two-month period immediately after the date of lodging, it is helpful to set these dates out in the covering letter to the Tribunal. For more on listing, see chapter 7.

CHAPTER 4

Before the hearing

Obtaining more information about the claim or the defence

Further and better particulars

In order to maximise your chances of mounting a successful claim or defence, you need to make sure that you understand exactly what the other party's case is going to be at the hearing. Only then will you know which witnesses and which documents you will need to have available at the hearing.

If the Originating Application does not give very much detail of the Applicant's complaint, the Respondent should send in a skeleton Notice of Appearance within 21 days or request an extension of time by stating the reason for this request. The Respondent should then write to the Applicant, or his/her nominated representative as appropriate, asking for further and better particulars of the Applicant's complaint. Quite often, an Applicant who is unrepresented will simply say, for example, in the Originating Application that 'I was unfairly dismissed'. The sort of request for further and better particulars which the Respondent should make in that situation is covered in chapter 3.

Even if the statement of claim in the Originating Application seems quite detailed, it can often contain statements which are unclear. Take, for example, a claim of unfair dismissal involving poor performance, in which the Applicant states that 'I was told at a meeting that my performance was appalling and I would never improve'. The Respondent can, and should, ask a number of questions to clarify this allegation such as:

Of the allegation 'I was told at a meeting that my performance was appalling and I would never improve', please state:

- the date, time and place of this alleged meeting

- the name of the person you allege made this alleged statement

- the exact words you allege this person used when making this alleged statement.

It would *not* be appropriate for the Respondent then to ask the Applicant to state, for example, whether he/she admits that his/her performance was poor. That sort of question would not strictly speaking be a request for further and better particulars; it should instead be put to the Applicant in cross-examination at the hearing.

The Applicant is equally entitled to request further and better particulars of the Respondent's Notice of Appearance. In the above unfair dismissal example, a statement in the Notice of Appearance that 'the Applicant was warned on more than one occasion that his/her performance was falling below the standards expected' may invite a request as follows:

Of the allegation 'The Applicant was warned..., etc.', on each and every occasion, please state:

- when and by whom the Applicant was so warned

- the exact terms of such warnings

- full details of the 'standards expected'; what are these standards and who sets them.

This request may also be coupled with a request to inspect relevant documents, i.e., notes of meetings or conversations, relevant correspondence and any applicable disciplinary procedure or performance standards documentation (see 'Discovery/disclosure', below).

Always ask the other party (or their representative, as appropriate) to respond to you within a reasonable time. That is rarely going to be less than seven days and will more likely be fourteen or twenty-one days depending upon the length and complexity of the questions you are asking. It is therefore important that you make your request well before the date of the hearing.

If you do not receive a response to your request within a reasonable time, you should write to the Tribunal, enclosing a copy of your letter to the other party (or representative) and ask the Tribunal to issue an Order requiring them to comply with your request. The Tribunal has the power to do this under Rule 4 (see Appendix 6). The Tribunal does not have to issue an Order but will usually do so if they receive your request within a reasonable time prior to the hearing and they consider that the further and better particulars you are requesting are reasonable. There follows a list of some of the main reasons Tribunals have given in the past for refusing such a request:

- The request is not for particulars of grounds on which the opposing party relies or facts or contentions relevant thereto.

- Sufficient details of the case have already been given.

- The particulars sought are not relevant.

- They are not necessary for fairly disposing of the case or saving costs.

- They are a matter of evidence, in other words, they seek to obtain evidence which the party making the request would then rely on to prove his/her case.

- It is a request for particulars of an admission.

- The request is oppressive or made only to cast discredit on the opponent.

- The request is in the nature of cross-examination, e.g., stressing an aspect of the case for tactical reasons or arguing for a particular finding.

A common reason for refusing a request for further and better particulars is that it is made too late. Bear in mind that it might take the Tribunal seven days or more to process your request.

The Tribunal can also decide to order the production of further and better particulars itself.

It is also possible for you to submit voluntary further and better particulars of your claim or defence. It would be sensible to do this if you have only been able to submit a skeleton Originating Application or Notice of Appearance because, for example, you were up against the time limit or waiting to receive further and better particulars of the Applicant's claim. Or, you might want to correct something in the documents you have already submitted. Write to the Tribunal explaining that you would like to submit further and better particulars of your claim or defence as appropriate, explain your reasons and set out those particulars in an attachment to your letter. Usually, the Tribunal will accept further particulars unless, for example, the Tribunal receives them from the Applicant outside the initial time limit for submission of that claim and it takes the view that the Applicant is seeking fundamentally to alter the nature of his/her case.

Written answers/interrogatories

You may also, before the hearing, ask the other party to give you a written answer to any question you ask, if the answer might help to clarify any issue likely to come up at the hearing and it is likely to assist matters if the answer is available before the hearing. This type of question is also known as an interrogatory.

So, in the example above concerning the dismissal for alleged poor performance, the Respondent might like to ask the Applicant the following question:

> *Do you confirm or deny that you received, at the commencement of your employment, a copy of the company's performance management procedure?*

The purpose of asking this question is so that the Respondent can understand whether or not he/she will need to bring a copy of this procedure to the hearing and prove the Applicant has been given it before. It is a question to which the Respondent does not know the answer, where the Applicant's response will assist the Respondent's preparation for the hearing.

You should not, however, be tempted to submit requests for written answers to questions where you do in fact know the answer and which should therefore be put to the other party in cross-examination at the hearing. So, for example, in this scenario the Respondent should not ask the Applicant for a written answer to the following question:

Do you confirm or deny that at a performance appraisal six months prior to your dismissal, your line manager informed you that your performance was failing in a number of respects?

if you already know, and can prove, that that is in fact what happened.

Again, you should ask the other party (or his/her representative as appropriate) to respond within a reasonable time. If they do not do so, you may ask the Tribunal for an Order requiring them to comply. Again, you need simply to write to the Tribunal, enclosing a copy of your letter containing the questions, explaining that you have not had a response and asking for the Order. The Tribunal does not have to comply, but will usually do so if it considers that the request is reasonable and there is a reasonable amount of time left before the hearing for the party to comply. Again, the Tribunal can decide to issue an Order for written answers itself.

There a follows a list of some of the Tribunal's main reasons for refusing an Order for interrogatories:

- The questions must be necessary for fairly disposing of the matter or saving costs.

- Questions which relate only to credibility are not allowed.

- They must relate to facts, the existence (or non-existence) of which is relevant to the existence of facts directly in issue, e.g., to get an admission of something which the party has to prove.

- There must be precise points on which information or admission is sought.

- No fishing, i.e., questions are not allowed which do not relate to any matter in question.

- Questions are not allowed where the object is to obtain an admission of a fact which can be proved by a witness who will in any case be called at the trial and, therefore, the interrogatory will not save but add to costs.

- Nor where it is plain that no admission can be obtained, e.g., where, in his/her Statement of Claim, the Applicant has already denied the allegation which is contained in the question.

- They will not be allowed to secure an admission of a fact solely within the knowledge of the party applying.

- Nor for securing admission of a fact or truth of which is a matter of opinion, e.g., what caused the accident?

- Oppressive interrogatories will not be allowed, e.g., interrogatories which seek to obtain admissions of all the statements in the pleadings of the party applying.

If the Tribunal has ordered the production of written answers, it must take account of those written answers in the same way as it takes account of any representations in writing which have been made to the Tribunal prior to the hearing. The Tribunal has a discretion, in this respect, as to the weight which it is prepared to attach to the content of any such documentation. The degree of weight it will be prepared to attach will depend upon the facts of each case. Note, however, that if written answers have been supplied by one party to the other voluntarily (not because they have been ordered to do so) the Tribunal does not necessarily have to take any account of those answers at all. In practice, however, Tribunals usually are prepared to consider written answers, as part of the evidence before the Tribunal, whether supplied voluntarily or pursuant to an order.

Discovery/disclosure

This is the process whereby both parties disclose to each other documents on which they intend to rely at the hearing or which may be relevant to the other side's case. It normally occurs after the Notice of Appearance has been submitted.

Discovery involves the exchange of lists of all the documents which each party is disclosing and the other party can then apply to 'inspect' any of the documents listed. Usually, 'inspection' is given by the party's representative providing photocopies of the documents listed. Those copies cannot be used for any purpose other than the Tribunal proceedings and must remain confidential. Alternatively, a party may decide to inspect the original documents at the other party's workplace or the offices of their representative and take copies. This is normally arranged by mutual agreement between the parties or their representatives.

To commence the discovery process, it is necessary to write to the other party asking them for discovery of all documents relating to the case. A general request for discovery may look like this:

Please forward, within 14 days of the date of this letter, copies of the following documents:

- *any document on which you propose to rely at the hearing*

- *any other document which is relevant to the matters which are to be determined in these proceedings.*

Either party can, of course, also ask for specific documents which he/she believes the other party possesses and which are relevant to the case.

Unless an Order for discovery is made by the Tribunal, there is no duty to disclose documents to the other party. However, if either party chooses to make voluntary disclosure of any documents in their possession or power, they must not be unfairly selective in their disclosure. 'Power' means available to that party, e.g., documents held by their solicitor or by another person who is able to release them upon their instruction.

In the case of a Respondent, company documents available to or held by others within the company would fall within the meaning of 'possession or power'. For example, the discovery obligations apply to records kept by line managers as well as to the personnel file retained by Human Resources.

If you disclose documents in support of your case, you must not withhold from disclosure any further documents in your possession or power if there is a risk that the effect of withholding those documents may give a false or misleading impression as to the true nature of any disclosed documents. Therefore, if any document is voluntarily disclosed, any documents which are relevant to that document or which may affect the impression that the disclosed document gives to the other party should also be disclosed.

It is important, therefore, that no documentation relevant to the proceedings is destroyed. Note also that 'documents' include photographs, films, tapes and computer records, and will also include any informal notes or e-mails which are made by either party and which may be relevant to the proceedings.

If the other party will not voluntarily disclose documents on which he/she intends to rely or that you suspect there has only been partial disclosure, you can ask the Tribunal for an Order under Rule 4. There follows a list of reasons why a Tribunal might refuse such a request:

- Inspection is only allowed after issues have been defined and where the documents are material to these issues.

- It is allowed only against a party, not witnesses or a prospective party.

- Inspection should not be ordered on matters which go solely to cross-examination or where discovery would be oppressive or the evidence in question would not be admissible.

- Nor where it would be in breach of legal privilege, i.e., advice or requests for advice between a solicitor and client.

- Nor where it would be in breach of litigation privilege, i.e., where it relates to negotiations to settle the claim in advance of the hearing (see chapter 5).

- It must be necessary either for fairly disposing of the case or saving costs.

There is no automatic exemption for confidential information. If it is material to the issues, it should be disclosed. Where the material information is contained within a document which also details issues which are irrelevant to the case and/or confidential and/or commercially sensitive, you have the option of 'blackening out' or 'covering up' this information to leave only the material part. The same applies to inadmissible or privileged information incorporated in a larger document.

Tribunal Orders

When asking the Tribunal for an Order, in respect of further and better particulars, or written answers or discovery, you should always be reasonably certain that the Tribunal will comply with your request. The other party will receive a copy of the correspondence and if the Tribunal refuses your request they may feel that they have secured a 'victory', thus reinforcing their determination to continue with the case all the way to a hearing.

If either party fails to comply with a Tribunal's Order, without reasonable excuse, they can be liable, on summary conviction, to pay a fine. A statement to this effect, together with the amount of the fine, will be stated in the Order.

The Tribunal also has the power to strike out the whole or part of the Originating Application or Notice of Appearance, as the case may be and, where appropriate, bar the Respondent from defending the claim. The Tribunal must first give notice to the party who has failed to comply with the Order that a strike out or a debarring is considered, to give that party the opportunity to make representations as to why the Tribunal should not do so.

Variations of Orders

If the Tribunal writes to you ordering you to supply written answers to questions or further and better particulars and you consider that the terms of the order are onerous (e.g., because of the amount of or type of information you are asked to provide, or the time you are given to provide it) you may write to the Tribunal asking it to vary the Order or set it aside. It is important that you submit your request to the Tribunal within the time which you have been given to comply. The Tribunal will then notify the other party(s) to the case that you have made this request. You will need to set out full reasons for your request in your application. The Tribunal has the discretion as to whether to grant your request or not.

Interlocutory Hearings

Where a party refuses to comply with an Order under one of the above headings, or there is a dispute between the parties as to whether a request is properly made, the Tribunal may list an interlocutory hearing. The purpose of the hearing is to determine the issue in dispute and only one representative from each party will normally be required to attend to explain that party's position. The Tribunal will normally consist of the Chairperson sitting alone. This Chairperson may or may not be the one who eventually hears the full case.

It is important to appreciate that although the Tribunals generally have a broad discretion, they will be guided by the laws of the County Court in determining procedural matters of this nature. You should seek advice if you are unclear, particularly where potentially sensitive documents are in dispute.

Generally, where discovery is concerned, be prepared with a list of the material documents you have in your possession and power. If particular documents requested are no longer available then find out why. Every party has an obligation to retain and safeguard relevant documents and this should be made clear to all involved and all who may possess relevant records at the earliest stage. If the confidential nature of the documents is in dispute and 'blackening out' is challenged, take the original to the Tribunal so that the Chairperson may have sight of it to determine the issue.

Regarding requests for further and better particulars or written answers, be clear what you are asking and why it is relevant to your case, or, if you are the recipient of the request, why you believe it does not progress matters or is unreasonable/immaterial.

Many Tribunals will also issue 'directions' at interlocutory hearings as to how the matter should be progressed from that point, in terms of exchange of lists of documents or witness statements – see chapter 6.

Amendments to the Claim or Defence

You may, in certain circumstances, wish to amend your Originating Application (or Notice of Appearance, as applicable). There are several situations in which this might be necessary: you might only have been able to submit a skeleton Notice of Appearance within the 21 days allowed; you might, following a request for further and better particulars have obtained further information, making a change to the grounds on which you are making or defending the claim necessary; you might have received advice, following the submission of the Originating Application, making you aware that, for example, as well as an unfair dismissal claim you might also have a disability discrimination claim. In what circumstances can you make the necessary amendments?

The key consideration in this respect is whether or not the proposed amendment raises a new cause of action or not. If it does not but merely provides more information about the grounds of the claim (or defence), the Tribunal will have the discretion to grant that amendment and will generally do so.

If, however, the proposed amendment raises a new cause of action, the Tribunal has to apply the rules about time limits for the presentation of claims. In other words, if, for example, you seek to amend your original IT1 which claimed unfair dismissal by adding new information which effectively amounts to the making of a new disability discrimination claim, the Tribunal will have to consider whether you are in time to make a disability discrimination claim or not. If you are not in time, and if the Tribunal is not persuaded that it would be just and equitable to extend time, you will not be able to make the amendment you seek. Be aware that, for example, if your original claim was one of unlawful discrimination and you wish to raise a claim of victimisation at a later date, that amendment is likely to amount to the making of a new claim and if you are out of time your application may be refused.

When you write to the Tribunal with your application to amend the Originating Application or Notice of Appearance (as appropriate) it is most important that you clearly set out verbatim the terms of the amendment that you seek and its intended effect.

Finally, the Tribunal also has a discretion, at any stage of the proceedings, to amend (or strike out) any Originating Application or Notice of Appearance or anything in them, on the grounds that it is scandalous, frivolous or vexatious.

Joinder of Parties

A Tribunal can at any time, as a result of an application made to it or on its own initiative, direct that any person against whom any remedy is sought should be joined as a party to the case. It can give any consequential directions which it considers necessary. Likewise, the Tribunal can dismiss from the proceedings any party whom or which it appears to the Tribunal is not, or has ceased to be, directly interested in the subject matter of the Originating Application.

Where there is a dispute as to which party or parties are the proper Respondent to a claim, that matter should be sorted out at a preliminary hearing at which the Tribunal can hear the appropriate evidence and arguments. It is not appropriate for the Tribunal to try to resolve this issue at a directions hearing, at which it would not necessarily be able to hear the relevant evidence.

. . . .

CHAPTER 5

Settlements and remedies

Introduction

It is by no means inevitable that disputes will have to be resolved by the Employment Tribunal. It is more often than not possible to reach some form of settlement with the other side before the full merits hearing.

Are you willing to settle, and, if so, for how much?

A useful way of looking at the issues is to consider the main factors common to most cases.

If you are the Respondent

- How likely are you to be successful in defending the claim?

- What will be the likely award against you should you lose?

- How much money do you want to spend defending the claim?

- How much management time can you afford to devote to defending the claim?

- How principled do you feel about defending the claim?

- Will settling the claim send out the wrong message to other staff and potential claimants?

- What are the publicity implications of fighting?

- Are costs likely to be awarded against you if you lose (see below)?

- (If you are a public sector employer) Are there any internal or external compliance considerations in making a settlement offer?

If you are the Applicant

- How likely are you to be successful at Tribunal?

- What award can you expect if you are successful at Tribunal?

- How much money do you want to spend pursuing the claim?

- How much time and energy do you have to devote to pursuing the claim?

- How principled do you feel about fighting the claim?

- Are costs likely to be awarded against you if you lose (see below)?

While all these factors are important the key ones, for both the Applicant and Respondent, are likely to be the first three in the respective lists. As such, careful attention should be paid to them and they should be reassessed and updated each time new information comes to light, for example, from the settlement negotiations.

Having made an initial assessment you should be in a position to put a preliminary figure on the price you are prepared to pay, or accept, to achieve settlement. However, as noted above, this will have to be kept under review as and when further information comes to light.

Achieving settlement and formalising it

Assuming breach of one or more of the statutory rights (such as, unfair dismissal, race, sex or disability discrimination – see chapter 1) has been claimed there are only two ways of achieving a legally effective settlement, namely: (a) through ACAS; or (b) a compromise agreement, made with the other side. Although both methods involve negotiation with the other side, and will result in a formal written agreement, they do differ in a number of important respects and so will be dealt with separately. However, before doing this a number of preliminary points should be considered.

Preliminary considerations

Job market and adverts

Later in this chapter we explain that the assessment of the Applicant's damages involves calculation of their financial loss from dismissal to the hearing, and from the hearing to some time in the future. How far into the future the Tribunal will look when calculating the Applicant's loss will depend upon how long it considers it will take the Applicant to find alternative employment, bearing in mind the Applicant's duty to seek it. Therefore, during the settlement process pressure can be applied to the Applicant by the Respondent if it can be shown that there are suitable jobs in the area he/she is *not* applying for. Likewise if it can be shown that the employment market is especially buoyant, the Respondent could suggest that the Tribunal will not look too far into the future when assessing loss, and that any settlement figure should be reduced accordingly.

It is therefore prudent to keep an eye out for copies of job adverts so that they can be drawn to the Applicant's attention during the settlement process. Applicants should keep records of jobs they apply for.

On the other hand, if the job market is depressed the Applicant should argue the opposite in an attempt to ensure the increase of any offer that may be put forward.

Application for costs

Although exceptionally rare, it is possible for the Employment Tribunal to award costs against either the Applicant or the Respondent if they bring or defend a claim frivolously, vexatiously, abusively, disruptively or otherwise act unreasonably.

Reinstatement or Re-engagement

If the Applicant asks for reinstatement or re-engagement by ticking the relevant box on the ET1 the Tribunal must consider whether it should order it. Although very rare, it may be the last thing the Respondent wants and so might encourage them to settle at a higher figure, simply to avoid the risk.

Having considered these preliminary issues, you will be ready to make contact with the other side. You may either contact them direct or use ACAS.

ACAS

ACAS will be aware of the claim because, following receipt of the claim, the Tribunal will send a copy of it, together with a copy of the employer's reply, to ACAS who will appoint a conciliation officer who will be responsible for seeing whether a settlement can be reached. However, they cannot force the parties to settle.

At some point before the hearing that conciliation officer will write to the parties, introducing themselves and offering their help to achieve a settlement.

Use these early conversations to obtain further information about the strength or weakness of the opponent's claim, or to communicate particular strengths in your case to the other side. If you are the Respondent, this will include ascertaining whether the Applicant has found a new job, if so when and how much they are earning. This helps quantify the loss.

Once the above has been completed and the hearing date is approaching you should be ready to make an offer (it is generally best not to put an offer in too early, unless of course you have a hopelessly weak case). If the other side can be encouraged to put their offer forward first, so much the better because it will give a better idea of what you are up against (for example, how much the Applicant wants).

Of course, someone has to get the ball rolling. When doing so there are a number of approaches you may want to take depending on whether you are the Applicant or the Respondent. For example, the Respondent might want to pitch the offer very low to begin with, in an attempt to lower the expectations of the Applicant. On the other hand, the Applicant would want to ask for as much as possible.

It is a good idea to ensure that any offer made is realistic, for example (in a Respondent's case):

- if the claim in a very weak one, but for commercial reasons you have decided to try and settle it, consider a nuisance offer. Such offers will usually be in the region of £500; on the other hand

- if the claim has some merit your offer should reflect the risk and the value of the claim (these should already have been assessed) and should be relatively close to the final amount you are prepared to pay – how close will depend on the precise risks and value of the claim. This way you will not have to dramatically increase the offer later, which will undermine your position.

A variation on this would be to advise the ACAS officer what you feel is a reasonable settlement figure, and why. You can then seek an indication that they agree with you, and ask them to find out from the other side if such an offer would be accepted were it to be forthcoming. This should encourage a sensible response from the other side, which can be worked with until a settlement is reached.

Offers can then go back and forth until settlement or deadlock is reached. If it is deadlock consider a reassessment of the value of the claim and your exposure so as to enable you to decide whether to increase the offer or allow the negotiations to lapse.

From the Applicant's perspective very little would be done differently, except that you should normally not accept a nuisance settlement, unless the Respondent had said they will not negotiate and you do not wish to take the matter forward to a hearing.

COT3

Once an oral agreement has been reached the conciliation officer will offer to record the terms in a form known as a COT3. ACAS has its own standard wording.

Once the wording has been agreed the conciliation officer will prepare four copies and send them to the Applicant for signing. The Applicant will then forward them to the Respondent when they have done so. The Respondent then signs each one, and sends two back to ACAS and one to the Applicant, while retaining one for their records. It is at this point (i.e., signing) that the time limit for actually making a payment will usually begin to run. ACAS will then send one completed form to the Tribunal and one each to the Applicant and the Respondent. For all intents and purposes the matter is then at an end.

Clearly all of this will take a few days, therefore the worry might be that the other side changes their mind between verbally agreeing the settlement terms with the conciliation officer and signing. However, you need not worry because an oral agreement made through a conciliation officer is binding.

Compromise agreement route

While ACAS can be very useful, you may not want to use or involve them if, for example, you are still able to negotiate objectively with the other side, and they with you, or because you want to achieve a swifter result by cutting out the 'middle man'. You may, of course, 'go-it-alone'. However, if you do you cannot then rely on ACAS to formalise any agreement you reach by drafting the COT3.

Once agreement is reached you will need to put in place a compromise agreement. If this is to be binding it is essential that it complies with the following requirements:

- it must be in writing

- it must relate to the particular complaint, or complaints, the Applicant is bringing, or is proposing to bring

- the Applicant must have received advice from an independent advisor as to the terms and effect of the agreement and, in particular, its effect on his/her ability to pursue his/her rights before an Employment Tribunal.

- there must be in place a policy of insurance covering any loss suffered by the Applicant as a result of that advice

- it must state that the conditions regulating compromise agreements are satisfied.

You may want to involve legal advisers to complete the Agreement. Applicants can use their trade union representatives. Respondents may feel confident enough to dispense with legal advice if the settlement is straightforward. Note that large settlements may need tax advice.

Other terms

- In either type of settlement you may want to consider including a confidentiality clause to prevent either party from disclosing the terms of the agreement.

- You may also wish to guarantee that you will not make disparaging remarks about each other.

- You may wish to agree on a form of reference which will be used. Respondents should ensure the contents of any references are true and not misleading or risk claims of negligent misstatements by future employers.

Remedies

Unfair Dismissal

For cases of unfair dismissal, compensation is calculated under two heads: the Basic Award and the Compensatory Award. In some instances an 'Additional Award' is also awarded.

Basic Award

The Basic Award is calculated by reference to the period during which the employee was continuously employed ending with the date of termination and allowing the following for each year employed:

- For each year when the employee was below the age of 22 – half a week's pay.

- For each year when the employee was below the age of 41 but not below the age of 22 – one week's pay.

- For each year when the employee was not below the age of 41 – one and a half week's pay.

The maximum allowable for a week's pay is [currently] £230 per week.

The maximum number of years to be taken into account when calculating the payment is 20. Therefore, the maximum basic award [currently] is £6,900 (£230 x 20 x 1.5).

Reducing the Basic Award

There are four grounds where the Basic Award may be reduced:

1   Where the conduct of the Applicant before dismissal, or where the dismissal was with notice, before the notice was given, was such that it would be just and equitable to reduce the Basic Award;

2   Where the Applicant has unreasonably refused an offer of reinstatement, the Tribunal will reduce (or further reduce) the Basic Award to such extent as it considers just and equitable having regard to that finding.

3   Where the employee has been dismissed for redundancy and received a redundancy payment.

The Compensatory Award

The Compensatory Award is calculated by reference to the loss the dismissed employee has in fact suffered because of the dismissal and is stated to be such amount as the Tribunal considers just and equitable in all the circumstances having regard to the loss sustained by the complainant in consequence of the dismissal in so far as that loss is attributable to action taken by the employer.

This may include expenses incurred (e.g., attending interviews) or benefits lost (e.g., loss of pension) as a result of the dismissal. In addition, the tribunal will usually award a nominal amount (often £200) to compensate the employee for loss of protection against unfair dismissal in his/her next employment. The Compensatory Award is subject to a maximum of £50,000. The Tribunal will award an amount to compensate the Applicant for losses until the date of the hearing and then future losses to compensate the Applicant for the period the Tribunal thinks it should take before a comparable job is found.

Reducing the Compensatory Award

There are a number of circumstances where the Tribunal can reduce the amount of Compensatory Award:

• The Applicant has failed to mitigate his/her loss by taking reasonable steps to obtain alternative employment. Alternatively, the Applicant has mitigated the loss by getting another job.

• Where the tribunal considers it just and equitable to limit the award – it may, for example, be just and equitable to make no award where the employer can show that the employee is in fact guilty of the misconduct alleged against him/her or other serious misconduct; or where they would or might have dismissed him/her fairly if there had been a thorough investigation.

• Where an Applicant has contributed to the dismissal, the Tribunal must reduce the Compensatory Award by such proportion as it considers just and equitable.

Three conditions must be met before a reduction for contributory fault is justified:

1 The Applicant is guilty of culpable conduct (i.e., conduct which is foolish, perverse or unreasonable).

2 The conduct must have contributed to the dismissal.

3 It must be just and equitable to reduce the Award.

• Payments by the employer to the Applicant which were due under the contract of employment – for example pay in lieu of notice. 'Ex gratia' payments may also be taken into account although the Tribunal does not have to do so.

Order of reductions

1 Offset any payment from the employer. At this stage exclude contractual severance to the extent it exceeds the basic award.

2 Deduct sum earned in mitigation.

3 Reduce the compensation by a percentage to reflect the chance the employee would have been dismissed in any event.

4 Make any deduction for contributory fault.

5 Finally, deduct contractual severance pay to the extent it exceeds the Basic Award.

Discrimination

Unlike unfair dismissal cases, there is no limit on the amount of compensation the Tribunal can award on a finding of race, sex or disability discrimination.

When calculating the amount of compensation, two factors will apply. The first relates to the loss suffered by the Applicant. The successful claimant should be put, so far as is possible, in the same position that they would have been in if the discrimination had not occurred and can include such items as present and future loss of earnings. This is particularly so where, for example, a woman having been dismissed for a reason connected with her pregnancy finds it harder to obtain the same or similar employment. Any mental or psychological injury suffered as a consequence will also be compensated (see chapter 10).

Secondly, the compensation may include a sum to reflect injury to feelings. Compensation should be compensatory and not punitive. An award of less than £500 for injury to feelings is likely to be perverse.

An injury to feelings award can include an award for aggravated damages if the treatment by the employer was malicious, exceptional or premeditated.

Other Remedies

If the Employment Tribunal finds that a complaint of unfair dismissal is well-founded, it should consider and may order reinstatement or re-engagement of the dismissed employees.

Reinstatement

An order for reinstatement is an order that the employer shall treat the complainant in all respects as if he/she had not been dismissed.

If an order for reinstatement is made, the Applicant is restored to his/her former job, and treated as if he/she had not been dismissed. A successful Applicant must be given the same job title, pay and back pay, together with those benefits which he/she would have received, had he/she not been dismissed. This is subject to any improvement in terms to which the Applicant would have been entitled had he/she not been dismissed.

When deciding whether to make an order for reinstatement, the Tribunal must consider:

•   whether the complainant wishes to be reinstated; if so,

•   whether it is practicable for an employer to comply with an order for reinstatement; and

•   whether in light of any contributory action by the complainant it will be just to grant the order.

Re-engagement

An order for re-engagement is a more flexible remedy than reinstatement. An order for re-engagement is defined as an order, on such terms as the Tribunal may decide, that the complainant be engaged by the employer, or by a successor of the employer or by an associated employer, in employment comparable to that from which he/she was dismissed or otherwise suitable employment.

The order for re-engagement may not need to be with the employer who dismissed the Applicant but with a successor or associated employer and it may involve a different job to that previously held by the Applicant provided that the new job is comparable to that from which he/she was dismissed. A Tribunal may not order re-engagement on terms substantially more favourable than the terms of the former job.

The same considerations apply when making an order for re-engagement as apply to reinstatement.

Failure to reinstate or re-engage

If circumstances have changed since the request for re-engagement or reinstatement, the employee's refusal to accept the reinstatement or re-engagement may be reasonable. However, if it is not and the employee unreasonably prevents the order being complied with, the Tribunal must take that conduct into account as a failure by the employee to mitigate his/her loss when determining any compensatory award.

If an employer does not comply with the order for reinstatement or re-engagement and cannot show that it was not practicable to comply with the order, then in addition to the usual compensation (Basic and Compensatory) the Tribunal will award additional compensation.

Additional Award

When calculating the Additional Award, maximum and minimum awards apply and range from 26 to 52 weeks' pay (current weekly pay being capped at £230, subject to change). Therefore, the Additional Award can range from £5,980 to £11,960. In determining the appropriate figure, the Tribunal has a wide discretion and the award is dependent upon the merits of the case. However, the Additional Award is not intended to cover something which is adequately and properly covered by the Compensatory Award, but merely to cover any additional loss suffered by the failure to reinstate or re-engage and conduct of the employer in failing to reinstate or re-engage must also be taken into account. Also, the Tribunal is entitled to take account of the extent to which the Applicant failed to mitigate his/her loss. An *ex gratia* payment by the employer which does not exhaust the Basic and Compensatory Award may also be offset against the Additional Award.

CHAPTER 6

Preliminary Hearings

Type of Preliminary Issue

The Tribunal rules

A Tribunal (often in the form of a Chairperson sitting alone) may, either on the application of a party, or of its own motion:

- hear and determine any issue relating to the entitlement of a party to bring or contest the proceedings (i.e., preliminary issues)

- conduct a pre-hearing review, or

- give directions.

Preliminary issues

A preliminary hearing may take place 'at any time before the hearing of an Originating Application'. It is usually held on a date before the main hearing of the complaint but it will sometimes be held on the date fixed for the main hearing but before the hearing on the merits.

The tribunal may decide to hold a preliminary hearing either upon the application of a party or of its own motion. If a party wishes to apply for a preliminary hearing, it should write to the Tribunal to request one. The party's letter must state the name of the proceedings, i.e., *Mr Bloggs v. ABC Limited*, and the Tribunal case number which is quoted on all correspondence from the Tribunal. The letter must also set out the grounds for the application. If the Tribunal agrees, it will write to all the parties confirming its intention to hold a preliminary hearing and the reason for that hearing. A date will then be set.

The rule provides for written representations and oral arguments to be advanced at a preliminary hearing but not for evidence to be given. In practice, however, evidence is normally heard and parties should attend the hearing with any witnesses on whom they depend.

The Employment Appeal Tribunal (EAT) and Court of Appeal have urged Tribunals to hold preliminary hearings sparingly. Experience shows that it is often quicker and cheaper to find all the facts first and then resolve the legal issues.

The power to consider preliminary issues covers any question that relates to the entitlement of an Applicant to present a complaint; for example, whether the complaint has been made in time, whether the Applicant had the necessary qualifying period of continuous employment, whether he/she was dismissed or resigned. These may be described as objections to the Tribunal's jurisdiction. However, the power to consider preliminary issues is not confined just to jurisdictional issues although the practice of deciding preliminary points of law should only be used exceptionally in clear and simple cases. Preliminary points of law are too often treacherous shortcuts. Usually it is not desirable for issues of law to be determined in isolation without evidence having been given and findings made on the material facts. In every case, where a preliminary issue will involve hearing evidence that substantially overlaps with the evidence on the substantive complaint, it is preferable that there should be only one hearing to determine all matters in dispute. The essential criterion for deciding whether or not to hold a preliminary hearing is whether the issue is capable of being determinative of the whole case: described by the EAT in one case as a 'knockout point'.

Pre-hearing reviews

A Tribunal may, either on the application of the party or of its own motion, conduct a pre-hearing review to consider (a) the contents of the Originating Application and Notice of Appearance, (b) any representations in writing and (c) any oral argument advanced by or on behalf of a party. Again, a party's application should state the title of the proceedings and the Tribunal's case number.

Notice must be given to the parties in advance of any such review giving them the opportunity to submit written representations and to advance oral argument at the review. No evidence will be heard, although documents such as the minutes of the disciplinary and appeal hearings and the letter of dismissal may well be relevant. If the Tribunal decides that it cannot form a view on the case without hearing oral evidence, then it will refuse a request for a pre-hearing review, and the Tribunal will write to tell you.

Pre-hearing reviews are often conducted by a Chairperson sitting alone. If on a pre-hearing review the Tribunal considers that the arguments put forward by a party have no reasonable prospect of success it may order him/her or it to pay a deposit of an amount not exceeding £150 as a condition of being permitted to continue to take part in the proceedings. The Order will contain summary reasons for the decision. But, before making an Order, the Tribunal must ascertain the ability of the party to comply with the Order when determining the amount of the deposit.

If an Order is made, the Tribunal must also explain to the party against whom the Order is made that he/she may have an award of costs made against him/her if his/her contentions are unsuccessful at the substantive hearing and that he/she could lose his/her deposit.

The deposit must be paid to the tribunal within 21 days beginning with the day when the Order is sent to the party. There are conflicting decisions of the EAT regarding what is meant by 'sent'. One says it is the date the document is sent to the parties, which date will be recorded on the document whereas others say that it is the date when the written order is deemed to have been effected in the ordinary course of post. A first-class letter will be deemed to have been served unless the contrary is proved on the second working day after posting. There is a discrepancy between the decisions of two days. Needless to say, aim to meet the first deadline on the basis you may then have some slippage.

This period may be extended by a further fourteen days if the party ordered to pay the Tribunal asks for an extension. If the deposit is not paid in time the Originating Application or Notice of Appearance (or that part of it to which the order relates) will be struck out: there is no discretion.

No member of the Tribunal conducting a pre-hearing review may sit on the Tribunal at the substantive hearing.

The pre-hearing review was introduced to eliminate hopeless cases by putting a party on risk as to costs.

The deposit will be returned to the party in three situations:

1   if he/she withdraws before a hearing

2   if he/she continues to a hearing and wins (which happens in only 15% of such cases); or

3   if he/she fails at the hearing but does not have an award of costs made against him/her.

A Tribunal can only give a costs warning if it considers that the contentions of a party (Applicant or Respondent) have no reasonable prospect of success. The phrase 'no reasonable prospect of success' requires a higher degree of certainty of failure than the test 'unlikely to succeed'. This stringent standard is reflected in the fact that deposits are ordered in something less than half of applications made.

Payment of the deposit is effected when a cheque is delivered to the Tribunal subject to it being honoured in due course. It is not a condition that the cheque is cleared within the 21-day period.

The making of a striking out Order is not a 'decision' and so cannot be reviewed although the Tribunal's power to give directions is wide enough to include the power to set aside or revoke a striking out Order wrongly made. For example, where the party claims he/she has not received the Order until a later date and missed the 21-day deadline, the Tribunal will order a directions hearing before a full Tribunal to determine whether he/she received the Order less than 21 days before he/she paid the deposit and, if not, whether or not time should be extended.

Directions

A Tribunal may at any time, whether on an application by a party or of its own motion, give directions on any matter arising in connection with the proceedings. An application by a party for directions is made by notice to the Tribunal, stating the title of the proceedings and setting out the grounds for the party's application. Directions can either be given at a hearing or on written application without a hearing. In the latter case, a party against whom an Order is made is entitled to apply to vary or discharge the Order.

The rationale for Tribunals giving directions orders is that all interlocutory stages of a particular case should be kept within the tight control of the Tribunal. It also recognises that a more formal approach to pleadings and procedures is desirable in more complicated cases. However, some Tribunals have adopted the practice of holding directions hearings by telephone conference.

Directions can be given on a wide variety of matters. They may deal with particular matters as they arise in a case or they may be used to map out the future course of the proceedings. Common directions are for the exchange of witness statements and for discovery and inspection. Some Tribunals adopt the practice of issuing automatic directions concerning matters such as agreeing a bundle of documents and preparing witness statements.

The EAT encourages the use of directions hearings, particularly in complex cases such as discrimination and equal pay cases. Directions orders are increasingly a feature of more commonplace applications for unfair dismissal.

Interim relief

In some dismissal cases, the Tribunal (usually in the form of a Chairperson sitting alone) can order that the contract of employment continues from the date of dismissal until the termination of the case; in effect, treating the employee as suspended rather than dismissed.

The right to claim such interim relief is confined to cases where the principal reason for dismissal is alleged to be the Applicant's involvement in specified trade union matters or health and safety at work, or that he/she made a protected disclosure under the Public Interest Disclosure Act 1998 (i.e., as a 'whistleblower').

The application can be made on the IT1 form or at a different time. However, it must be made within seven days of the date of termination of employment. The Tribunal must decide applications for interim relief as soon as practicable so postponements are most unlikely.

If the Applicant is claiming infringement of his/her union rights he/she must also produce a certificate signed by an official of the relevant union confirming that the Applicant was or proposed to become a member of the union and there were reasonable grounds for supposing that the reason for dismissal was union involvement.

At the hearing of the application the Tribunal must decide whether it appears likely (i.e., on a balance of probability) that the Applicant was dismissed for the alleged reason. Usually witnesses are not called but a submission is made on behalf of the Applicant and documents are referred to.

The Tribunal must ask the Respondent if they, or it, is willing to reinstate or re-engage the Applicant. If the Respondent refuses, or the Applicant reasonably refuses re-engagement, the Tribunal will make an order for continuation of the contract of employment until determination of the case.

CHAPTER 7

Preparing the Case

Listing hearings

It is the Tribunal's regional Chairperson's responsibility to fix the date, time and place of the hearing of the claim. Thereafter, the Tribunal sends each party a notice of hearing together with information and guidance as to attendance at the hearing, witnesses and the bringing of documents, representation by another person and the making of written representations.

The Tribunal must send out the notice of the hearing at least 14 days prior to the date the hearing is to take place. In practice, the parties usually have far more notice than this of the hearing date (although where, for example, another case has been withdrawn from the list, giving the Tribunal an opportunity to list another case in its place, you may find that you get little more than the 14 days).

If for any reason the hearing date is inconvenient for you (because, for example, one of your witnesses is on holiday or has a pressing business engagement that day) you may apply to the Tribunal asking for a postponement. You must make your application within 14 days of the date of the Tribunal's letter informing you of the hearing date. If you make your application outside this time-frame the Tribunal will only consider it in exceptional circumstances.

The Tribunal, in considering your application, will have regard to the reasons you put forward for a postponement. It is likely to agree the application if the reason is that one or more of your witnesses will be unable to attend the hearing (although it is not unknown for tribunals to require evidence of unavailability (e.g., copies of plane tickets!) The unavailability of your representative will normally not be a sufficient reason for needing a postponement.

As well as setting out full reasons for your application, it is also courteous to provide the Tribunal with dates over the next few months on which you and your witnesses will be unavailable to attend the hearing so that the Tribunal can use these as a guide, should they decide to postpone and re-list.

Your witnesses

Which witnesses?

You will need to give careful thought, well before the hearing, as to which people you will need to call as witnesses to the hearing. The Tribunal will normally only be prepared to consider evidence from individuals who have first-hand knowledge of the events in question. Furthermore, the Tribunal will normally not be prepared to consider that first-hand evidence in writing alone. The individuals themselves must be present at the hearing to give evidence so that they can be cross-examined by the other party (or their representative if they have one) and the members of the Tribunal themselves.

If one of your witnesses really cannot attend, for example, because he/she has moved abroad or is ill and on balance you do not wish to apply for a postponement, the Tribunal does have the discretion to admit the written statement. If the statement is admitted, the statement will not be given as much weight as evidence in person, because the other party will have no opportunity to challenge it by way of cross-examination. The County Court rules confirm that the statement will be treated as hearsay evidence (i.e., second-hand evidence), although these rules do not bind the Tribunal. The other party has the opportunity to object to the Tribunal to the admission of a statement, which will be important if the evidence is crucial and contested. The Tribunal will decide the matter exercising its discretion.

Respondents should make sure that they at least have available every individual who has made any decision in the events relevant to the Applicant's claim, usually the managers who dismissed and heard the appeal. You may also need to ensure the attendance of others, such as an investigating officer or Human Resources manager (although you may find, on the day, that not all of them have to give evidence).

Witness statements

It is now routine for witnesses to present their evidence in chief (that is, their version of events) at the hearing in a written statement. The witness, having been asked to take the oath or affirm, may be asked to read out their statement (copies of which would be provided to the other party's representative if appropriate and the members of the Tribunal). The witness would then be asked questions about the content of the statement and any other matters relevant to his/her evidence, in cross-examination. Alternatively, it is becoming increasingly common for statements to be 'taken as read'. This means the Tribunal members will read the statements for themselves as the evidence in chief. The witness may be asked a few additional questions by his/her representative, but will then be cross-examined. This saves time and hence costs. Chapter 8 contains more detail about these aspects.

You will therefore need to ensure that each witness has prepared a statement. It is better that they do this rather than you. The evidence will then be set out in their own words and there is less of a risk that they will contradict themselves in cross-examination. It might be useful, however, for you to discuss the general content of their statement with them first, to ensure they cover all the issues which are likely to arise in the other party's evidence and which they can address.

The witness statement should:

1   begin by stating the witness's name, home address and date of birth

2   deal with preliminary matters, explaining the witness's role in the organisation, how long they have been in that role, what their responsibilities are, who they report to and, if relevant any professional or other qualifications

3   set out the witness's version of events from the beginning to the end of their involvement

4   stick to the facts and not include any opinions (unless, for example, the witness is giving an expert opinion and has the qualifications and experience to do so)

5   avoid including anything on which it is more appropriate for another individual to give first-hand evidence. Lengthy duplication of evidence in two or more statements can annoy the Tribunal (there is nothing to prevent a witness stating that he/she has read another's statement and agrees with his/her evidence)

6   refer to any relevant documents and include bundle page numbers (about which more is said below)

7   end with a confirmation by the witness that the evidence contained in the statement is true to the best of the witness's knowledge and belief.

Many Tribunals require the Applicant and Respondent to exchange copies of witness statements simultaneously prior to the hearing (usually seven days beforehand). They are particularly likely to do so if the case is complex, involves a number of witnesses and/or there is legal representation on both sides. If the Tribunal requires you to do this, it will write to you asking you to do so. If not, you should bring with you to the hearing sufficient copies of each statement for the Applicant (and representative), the witness and the three Tribunal members. If statements are to be taken as read, you may be asked to bring additional copies for any members of the press who attend the hearing.

Bear in mind that the Tribunal will almost certainly allow the witness, when giving evidence, to expand orally on the information contained in his/her witness statement.

Ensuring attendance of witnesses at the hearing

Normally the individuals you need to be present at the hearing will be willing to attend. Ensure that they know the date, time and place of the hearing and have a copy of any map or directions issued by the Tribunal showing how to get there. Tribunal proceedings normally start at 10.00 a.m. (sometimes 9.45 a.m. or 10.30 a.m.); it is sensible to ask your witnesses to arrive well in advance. There is a separate waiting room for Applicants and Respondents and these are usually open from about 9.00 a.m. It is always worth checking these details with the Tribunal concerned if you are unsure.

If, however, one or more of your witnesses tells you that they are not prepared to attend the Tribunal voluntarily (a trade union representative, for example) you can apply to the Tribunal for a witness order. You should write to the Tribunal explaining why you require the attendance of that person at the hearing and giving their name and address. If you do not know their home address it is usually acceptable for you to give their business address. Only witnesses based in the UK can be witness-summoned. If the Tribunal accepts your request, they will write to the individual directly (sending you a copy of the letter) requiring that individual to attend the hearing and warning them that if they do not do so they may be liable, on summary conviction, to pay a fine, the amount of which will be set out in the Order.

The Tribunal can either, on its own initiative or on the application of any party, make a witness order requiring the attendance of a witness at the hearing (as long as that person resides in Great Britain).

If you make an application to the Tribunal in this respect, the Tribunal will consider whether, on the facts of the case, the evidence which you say the witness will be able to present is sufficiently relevant. If you have applied for certain witness orders to be made and the Tribunal has declined to grant them on this ground, you will only be able to challenge the Tribunal's decision if you can show that it was unreasonable – that is, that the Tribunal made a mistake of law, misunderstood the facts, took into account irrelevant matters or failed to take into account relevant matters.

It is possible for the Tribunal, having heard evidence from the witnesses present at the hearing, to decide that it needs to hear evidence from further witnesses and to make orders appropriately. If, therefore, it appears to the Tribunal during the course of the hearing that its original decision not to make a witness order might be wrong, the Tribunal can always remedy the matter, adjourning the hearing if necessary.

The Tribunal will generally be reluctant to compel the attendance on the Applicant's behalf of any of the Respondent's employees, but if the evidence is important to your case, make the application stating why.

Bear in mind that if you call a witness to a hearing (either voluntarily or by means of a witness order) you can only examine them in chief (that is, you can only ask them for their version of events). You cannot cross-examine them.

Also, before asking the Tribunal for a witness order, consider carefully the wisdom of calling the witness at all. A reluctant witness is unlikely to assist your case. It is possible that the Applicant will call them, in which case you would be able to cross-examine them.

Preparing your bundle of documents

You will probably have a number of documents which you want to show the Tribunal at the hearing. Examples of the sorts of documents relevant to some Tribunal claims are found in chapter 3. See also chapter 4. Following the discovery process (which is described in chapter 4), you may also have received from the other party copies of a number of documents which will be produced at the hearing. It is important to ensure that these documents are set out properly in a bundle which the Tribunal, the parties and witnesses will find easy to follow at the hearing.

The first issue to consider is – who should prepare the bundles? Usually six bundles are required: one each for the Applicant and Respondent, one for the witness table and three for the tribunal. The bundle can be quite long (sometimes hundreds of pages!) and therefore expensive to produce. The best solution for a Respondent may be to try to agree with the Applicant that he/she produces the bundles but that the Applicant contributes half of the cost. If the Applicant refuses to agree to this and if the Applicant's documents are very extensive, it might be better for you to prepare your own bundle and let the Applicant prepare theirs. If the Tribunal directs that a single, composite bundle should be produced, however, both parties should co-operate to produce one.

When putting the bundle together, you should begin with the Originating Application, the Notice of Appearance, any further and better particulars of the claim or defence, any request for written answers and responses (if any) and your request for discovery of documents. Then you can incorporate all the paperwork on which you are going to rely (and that produced by the other party, if you have agreed to include it in your bundle) in order. Chronological order may be the most sensible, although this is not always the case. You need to ensure, above all, that as you call your witnesses, and as each of them refers to documents in the bundle in giving their evidence, that the Tribunal travels smoothly through the bundle. Tribunal members can become annoyed if they find themselves constantly going forward and back through a bundle.

When the documents are all in order, you should ensure that they are neatly numbered and that a table of contents, correctly corresponding to that numbering, appears on the front of each bundle.

You do not have to exchange bundles with the Applicant prior to the hearing but it is good practice to do so (at least seven days beforehand). The Tribunal will not normally require the parties to do so unless the case is unusually complex.

Written Representations

If you, or the other party, wish to submit representations in writing for the Tribunal's consideration at the hearing of the case, you (or they) must submit those representations to the Tribunal not less than seven days before the hearing and at the same time a copy must be sent to the other party.

If the written representations are submitted to the Tribunal prior to the seven days before the hearing, the Tribunal must consider those as part of the evidence at the hearing. If they are presented less than seven days prior to the hearing, the Tribunal has the discretion to consider them but cannot be required to do so.

If the Tribunal does consider them, it has discretion as to the weight if any to be attached to them. Bear in mind that if the written representations contain evidence which it would be possible for a witness to present at the hearing, the Tribunal may decide not to attach any weight to those representations at all. It would take the view that the witness should be present at the hearing so that he or she can give evidence on oath and can be questioned by the other party and by the Tribunal. In exceptional circumstances, however, tribunals will attach weight (although not as much weight as it attaches to witness evidence given in person) to representations where it is satisfied that there are good reasons why the relevant witness cannot attend and there are also good reasons why the hearing should proceed and not be adjourned to allow the attendance of that witness.

Preparation for remedies

Normally, the main hearing of the case will deal only with the question of liability, that is, whether the claim is proved or not. If the claim is proved, the hearing will then be adjourned to allow the parties to settle the question of remedy between themselves. Occasionally, however, the Tribunal will decide, following a finding that the claim is proved, to move straight into remedies.

The type of remedy which can be sought will of course depend on the claim which is being brought. In the case of unfair dismissal, for example, the Applicant can seek reinstatement, re-engagement and/or compensation. If the Applicant has indicated on the Originating Application that they are seeking one particular form of remedy, they can change their mind at the hearing. It is therefore important that you bring with you to the hearing sufficient information to enable you to deal with the question of remedy, whether you are making or defending a claim.

If, for example, you are an Applicant making an unfair dismissal claim you will need to bring with you all relevant evidence to enable you to explain to the Tribunal exactly what your loss as a consequence of the unfair dismissal has been in terms of lost earnings and expenses incurred as a direct result of the dismissal (e.g., in finding alternative employment). You also need to bring along a note of any state benefits received in the period from dismissal to the date of hearing. As you are under a duty to mitigate your loss, it would also be a good idea to bring along with you evidence that you have tried to comply with that duty and if you have found alternative employment, appropriate evidence of the income you are now receiving from your new job.

If you are a Respondent, and you foresee that you might have to resist a claim of reinstatement or re-engagement, you will need to produce appropriate supporting evidence showing why it is not practicable for such a remedy to be given. Relevant examples would include evidence of reorganisation following the Applicant's dismissal or evidence from the Applicant's old manager stating that there has been an irreconcilable breakdown in relationship between the manager and the Applicant and that it would not be possible for them to work together again. The Tribunal is not bound to concur with any such view but will take it into account. It would also be as well to bring along information as to the Applicant's pay and benefits at the time of the dismissal so that any information produced by the Applicant in this respect can be double-checked.

CHAPTER 8

At the Hearing

Upon arrival at the Tribunal

The representatives and the witnesses of all the parties should arrive at the tribunal in good time. For a 10.00 a.m. start, aim to be there between 9.00 a.m. and 9.30 a.m. Sign in at the Tribunal reception, where the Tribunal staff will tell you the Tribunal you are in and direct you to the appropriate waiting room. Applicants and Respondents have separate waiting rooms.

Prior to the hearing, the Tribunal clerk will speak to both parties in their waiting rooms. The clerk will ask each of the witnesses whether they wish to swear or affirm when they give their evidence. If you require any Holy Book other than the New Testament, you should tell the clerk. If you decide to affirm (without any Holy Book) your evidence still has the same weight.

The clerk will also collect the four bundles of documents for the Tribunal members and witness stand, and copies of the witness statements.

When the hearing is ready to start, the clerk will come to the waiting room to tell you. You should never walk directly into a Tribunal room without invitation, because the Tribunal may be having confidential discussions regarding the case.

In the Tribunal room

The Tribunal room will be set out with a long, probably elevated, table at one end for the three Tribunal members. In front of the Tribunal there will be a chair and table for the witness, which will either be facing the Tribunal or at right angles to it, plus a chair and table for the clerk. Next there will be tables where the representatives sit, and behind the representatives there will be seating for the witnesses waiting to be called, members of the public and any others interested in the proceedings.

It is important to appreciate that most hearings must be open to the public. The public and also members of the press can therefore come and go as they please. The only exceptions relate to cases concerning national security, or where the hearing may involve evidence which a witness cannot disclose without breaking the law, or breaking a confidence or (with some exceptions) where the disclosure of the evidence would cause substantial injury to the witness's business or the business he/she works for. Reporting restrictions may apply in cases of discrimination.

In the absence of these special circumstances, the decision of a Tribunal to sit in a room inaccessible to the public is unlawful and appealable.

The Tribunal is made up of three members, a legally qualified Chairperson and two laymembers being nominees of both sides of industry (i.e., from employers' groups and from employees' groups). Both laymembers will have considerable industrial relations and employment experience. For further information, see chapter 1.

The Chairperson should be addressed as Sir or Madam. When the Tribunal members enter or leave the room, everyone will be expected to stand.

In the Tribunal room, the Applicant's team sits on the right-hand side of the room and the Respondent's sit on the left. Always ensure that everyone, witnesses and representatives and supporters, have switched off their mobile telephones. Witnesses and supporters must also appreciate that the Tribunal is essentially a court room. Talking, sniggering and other distractions will not be tolerated and will incur the Tribunal's displeasure.

The hearing

At the start

The Chairperson will start the hearing by welcoming the parties and reviewing with the representatives any preliminary issues and how the evidence will be presented.

Preliminary issues at this stage may consist of a preliminary hearing before the full hearing on the merits (see chapter 6) or matters such as corrections or minor amendments to the pleadings.

Order of evidence

The order in which the evidence is presented will depend on where the burden of proof lies. The party on whom the burden of proof lies (at least initially) will normally be required to present their evidence first. A snapshot of where the burden lies in common cases is set out below:

* unfair dismissal – Respondent (to demonstrate potentially fair reason for the dismissal)
* constructive dismissal – Applicant (to demonstrate a fundamental breach of contract entitling him/her to resign)
* discrimination – Applicant (to demonstrate less favourable treatment on the ground of his/her sex, race or disability as appropriate (direct discrimination) or the imposition of a condition or requirement with which a considerably smaller proportion of his/her race or sex could comply (indirect discrimination))

- breach of contract – Applicant (to demonstrate breach of contract and loss flowing from the breach).

In some cases, the burden will be split; for example, a claim of unfair dismissal where the Applicant claims that he/she was selected for redundancy on the ground of his/her race or sex. In such a claim, the dispute centres initially on the reason for the Applicant's dismissal, i.e., whether it was a discriminatory reason and, if not, whether it was a potentially fair reason. Then the focus will be on whether it was fair to dismiss for that reason; the burden lies on the parties equally. It makes sense therefore for the Respondent to give its evidence first to establish its reason for the dismissal.

Opening statements

Most Tribunals used to allow opening statements summarising the case. This would cover the type of case, what each side seeks to prove and any facts not in dispute. The making of opening statements is now very rare. Tribunals prefer to review the pleadings and then to hear the evidence straight after dealing with the preliminary matters. If the case you are dealing with is particularly complex, or the pleadings do not adequately explain the case, then you may wish to offer to make an opening statement. It will then be up to the Tribunal whether they wish you to do so.

Procedure at the hearing

The Tribunal has a broad discretion regarding how to handle the hearing. The Tribunal rules state that:

> The Tribunal shall, so far as it appears to it appropriate, seek to avoid formality in its proceedings and shall not be bound by any enactment or rule of law relating to the admissibility of evidence in proceedings before the courts of law. The Tribunal shall make such enquiries of persons appearing before it and witnesses as it considers appropriate and shall otherwise conduct the hearing in such manner as it considers most appropriate for the clarification of the issues before it and generally to the just handling of the proceedings.

Subject to the above, at the hearing of an Applicant's claim each party is entitled to give evidence, to call witnesses, to question any witnesses and to address the Tribunal.

Presentation of the Evidence

Evidence in chief

As explained in chapter 7, most tribunals require witnesses to attend with a written witness statement, containing their evidence. The witness will then either be asked to read the statement, or the Tribunal will read it for themselves and take the evidence as read. The witness's own representative may be allowed to ask a few additional questions. You should always try to include all of the material evidence in the witness statement, in case the Tribunal does not give you much time for additional questions. Some Tribunals are reluctant to allow them.

Witnesses asked to read the statement should read slowly and clearly and address their evidence to the Tribunal members. Each of the Tribunal members will have a copy of the statement to follow.

The statement may refer to specific documents in the bundle of documents and it is helpful to include the page numbers in the written statement. The representative should ask the witness to pause where a document is relevant to the evidence and direct the Tribunal to the appropriate page.

The Tribunal members will usually wish to read the document for themselves, rather than for the witness or representative to do so. Where the document is long, it can be helpful to direct the Tribunal to the relevant paragraph. If the original of the document is disputed, ask the witness to explain who wrote it, in what circumstances and, where minutes of meetings are concerned, whether they believed them to be an accurate record of events.

The content of the statement will depend on the nature of the case. A basic framework is suggested at chapter 7. In collating witness evidence, a party should focus on what it needs to demonstrate to make out its claim or defence. If the Respondent's defence is that the Applicant was dismissed for misconduct arising from an occasion of unauthorised absence, for example, lengthy detail about historical performance issues may well be irrelevant. The Respondent's evidence should cover the reason for dismissal, i.e., why the witness believed the misconduct occurred, what investigation took place and what the findings were and on what basis and why the witnesses believe that dismissal was the appropriate sanction. On the latter point, recent disciplinary history, length of service and mitigating factors raised by the Applicant will all be relevant.

Cross-examination

After the witness has completed his/her evidence in chief, the other party or that party's representative has the opportunity to cross-examine the witness. The process of cross-examination is to challenge a witness's evidence where it is disputed by the other party, and to put forward the other party's version of events.

Cross-examination should be focused on the relevant issues and not be distracted on disputed evidence which has no bearing on the circumstances of the claim.

When cross-examining you must put your party's specific allegations to the appropriate witness. If, for example, you are representing the Applicant and the Applicant is planning to allege that his/her line manager behaved in a certain way, then you must put that to the line manager in question to give him/her the opportunity to comment.

Failure to do so may lead the Tribunal to discount the Applicant's evidence on that issue.

Witnesses should speak clearly and slowly when giving evidence as the Tribunal members will be taking notes of what is said.

Witnesses should also remember to be polite and resist appearing uncooperative or annoyed when being cross-examined. They should answer the question put to them, not the question which they think should have been asked, or the question they would prefer to have been asked. They should not be afraid of silences between questions and should not be tempted to keep talking if they have nothing further to add.

Re-examination

Once cross-examination of a witness has been completed, the Tribunal members may ask the witnesses their own questions.

After that, the Applicant's own representative will be able to ask further questions, but only where they arise from the questions put in cross-examination or by the Tribunal members. Re-examination is not a second opportunity to give further evidence. Instead, it is an opportunity for a witness to clarify issues which may have become clouded during cross-examination.

Completion of a party's evidence

When a party has presented the evidence of all of its witnesses present, the Tribunal will ask the representative if that completes the party's case. Normally the answer will be yes. There may be rare circumstances where cross-examination or the Applicant's case presented in Tribunal gives rise to issues to which the witnesses present are unable to answer, in which case you may wish to seek leave from the Tribunal to call additional witnesses. If so, tell the Tribunal at the earliest possible stage that this is what you propose to do so there is as little disruption to the hearing as possible. Once all of your witnesses have completed their evidence, that is the end of your case and it will be the other party's opportunity to present their evidence. Submissions follow the completion of all the evidence.

Closing submissions

Each party will be permitted to give closing submissions. The party who has the burden of proof will give their submissions last.

The closing submissions should summarise material and legal issues and the evidence upon which that party is relying in support of its case. The evidence mentioned must include that given in cross-examination and as such you will need to update any pre-prepared submissions as the hearing progresses.

The submissions should end by explaining what you are seeking, i.e., the findings you are asking the Tribunal to make. Obviously each party wants to succeed and will be asking the Tribunal to rule in its favour. The Respondent defending the claim should also consider whether it should put forward alternative arguments, in case its defence does not succeed. For example, Respondents should consider whether to ask for a reduction in compensation in view of the Applicant's contributory fault, or a finding that the Applicant would not have remained in employment for much longer in any event and that the compensation should be reduced accordingly. The latter is known as a 'Polkey' reduction. This may be applied if the Tribunal considers that there was a defect in the dismissal procedure (rather than in the substantive decision to dismiss), and that had the defect not occurred, the Applicant may in any event not have kept his/her job. The reduction is normally expressed in the form of a percentage, i.e., the percentage chance of the Applicant remaining in employment.

The decision

Once submissions are completed, the Tribunal will retire to make their decision (either unanimously or by a majority) and either return to the hearing room to announce the decision orally or to tell you that they need further time and that the decision will be reserved.

If the decision is reserved, the Tribunal will arrange to meet in private after the hearing to discuss the case and will then send a written decision to both parties within 4–6 weeks.

The Tribunal's written decision will state whether the reasons for the dismissal are in summary or extended form. Decisions in discrimination cases are given in extended form. Other cases may receive summary reasons, unless a party requests extended reasons. Such a request can be made either at the hearing itself, or in writing afterwards. The request must be made either before summary reasons are sent to the parties or within 21 days of receiving summary reasons. The Tribunal may also send extended reasons where it considers that summary reasons would not adequately explain the decision.

If a decision is given orally at the end of the hearing, the Tribunal may want to consider remedies at that point. That is why both parties need to be prepared to deal with the issues of reinstatement, re-engagement and compensation at the first hearing (see chapter 4). Alternatively, the Tribunal may prefer to adjourn and to have a separate hearing on compensation. This is often the preferred route and gives parties the opportunity to settle the case without a further hearing. A decision given orally will be confirmed in writing and signed by the Chairperson.

References to the European Court of Justice

It is possible in some cases related to European law that the Tribunal will not be able to make a ruling on the evidence without seeking guidance from the European Court of Justice (ECJ).

In these circumstances, the Tribunal can make an order referring the question to the ECJ for a preliminary ruling under Article 177 of the Treaty establishing the European Community.

Such an order can be appealed and if so, the reference will be made (if relevant) only after the appeal has been determined or otherwise disposed of.

Referrals to the ECJ generally take up to 2 years. Pending the decision of the ECJ, the Tribunal hearing will be stayed.

CHAPTER 9

The Decision, Costs and Appeals

Costs

A party cannot normally expect a Tribunal to award costs if they win nor will they generally be ordered to pay the other side's costs if they lose.

However there are four circumstances in which costs orders can be made:

1   *Unreasonable conduct*

The Tribunal can award costs if, in its opinion, a party (Applicant or Respondent) has in bringing or conducting the proceedings acted frivolously, vexatiously, abusively, disruptively or otherwise unreasonably.

'Frivolously' might cover cases where a party ought to have known that he/she had no prospect of success. An employee might act 'vexatiously' if he/she brought a hopeless case, not with any expectation of recovering compensation but out of spite to harass his/her employer or for some other improper motive. 'Abusively, disruptively' would cover a situation where a party had been abusive during the course of a Tribunal hearing or had attempted to disrupt it. 'Otherwise unreasonably' might cover, for example, an Applicant's unreasonable behaviour in pursuing a claim knowing that another employee dismissed for the same offence on the same day had failed in his/her dismissal claim.

Costs can be awarded against Respondents as well as Applicants. However, costs orders against Respondents are less likely and a Respondent ought not to be penalised for having unsuccessfully defended proceedings brought against him/her/it provided the defence was conducted reasonably. Tribunals cannot award costs against Respondents for their conduct leading to the dismissal: only for the way in which they react to an Applicant's claim.

2   *Failure to reinstate*

The Tribunal has specific power to award costs and expenses if:

(a)   the Applicant has expressed the wish at least seven days before the hearing of the complaint to be reinstated or re-engaged; or

(b)   the proceedings arise out of the Respondent's failure to permit the Applicant to return to work after an absence due to pregnancy and the proceedings have to be postponed due to the Respondent's failure, without special reason, to adduce reasonable evidence as to the availability of the Applicant's job, or suitable employment.

3   *Costs of postponed hearings*

The Tribunal has the discretion to award costs against the party whose conduct leads to adjournment or postponement of the hearing. There is no requirement that the party should have acted unreasonably.

4   *After a deposit order*

In a case where a deposit was ordered by the Tribunal at a pre-hearing review (see chapter 6), the Tribunal hearing the substantive claim must consider whether to award costs against the party on the ground that the party conducted the proceedings unreasonably in pursuing the matter to a full hearing. The second Tribunal's reasons for its decision must be 'substantially the same' as the reasons at the first Tribunal in ordering a deposit. Even then it does not follow automatically that costs must be awarded.

Amounts to be awarded as costs

An order for costs can be made in one of three ways:

1   A specified sum not exceeding £500; or

2   A sum which has been agreed between the parties; or

3   Costs to be taxed (i.e., assessed by the County Court) when, generally, the party in whose favour the order is made will recover all their costs reasonably incurred.

Witnesses allowances

Allowances are paid by the Secretary of State to parties and witnesses attending a Tribunal but rarely fully compensate the person for his/her loss of wages. Professional representatives are not entitled to receive an allowance.

Enforcement of Tribunal Award

Money awards

The Tribunals cannot enforce payment of their own awards. In order to obtain enforcement of an award the decision must be registered at the County Court in England, or the Sheriff Court in Scotland.

Application for registration is made by filing an affidavit (i.e., sworn statement) verifying the amount of the sum due and attaching a copy of the Tribunal decision.

Once the decision has been registered the sum is recoverable through the enforcement machinery of the County Court; for example, using the Bailiff, charging orders on property or attachment of earnings orders.

Non-money awards

In this instance, the Tribunal can enforce its own award, invariably by imposing a higher sum by way of compensation; for example, if a Respondent fails to comply with a reinstatement or re-engagement order.

Mistakes

Simple clerical mistakes in a decision of a Tribunal may be corrected at any time by the Tribunal Chairperson. The power is generally referred to as 'the slip rule'. It is restricted to clerical mistakes and arithmetical errors.

There is a more extensive power for Tribunals to review their own decisions in the following circumstances:

- the decision was wrongly made as a result of an error by the Tribunal

- a party did not receive notice of the proceedings or the hearing

- new evidence has become available since the hearing, the existence of which could not have been reasonably known or foreseen at the time of the hearing

- the interests of justice require a review; for example, where some procedural error has led to an erroneous decision or where the Compensatory Award was made on false evidence by the Applicant.

An application for a review can either be made orally at the hearing, or in writing to the Tribunal within 14 days after the date on which the decision was sent to the parties (time may be extended). The application must set out the grounds for seeking a review and a failure to do so is likely to lead to a refusal of the application on the ground that it has no reasonable prospect of success.

Appeals

Employment Appeals Tribunal

Appeals from Tribunals under all employment protection and discrimination legislation go to the Employment Appeals Tribunal (EAT). The EAT sits in London and Edinburgh and its decisions are binding on Tribunals. Appeals are heard by a judge and one member from each side of industry.

Right to Appeal

An appeal to the EAT lies only on a question of law, i.e., a misdirection, misapplication or misunderstanding of the law.

It is an error of law for a Tribunal to make a perverse decision, i.e. a decision for which there is no evidence in support.

A successful allegation of bias on the part of the Tribunal is an error of law because it is a breach of the rules of natural justice.

Time Limits for Appeal

The appeal must be lodged with the EAT, together with a copy of the Tribunal's decision, within 42 days of the date on which the full decision is sent to the parties. An application for an extension of time is possible but rarely granted.

Appeal Hearing

Provided the appeal has not been rejected at a preliminary stage on the grounds that it raises no arguable point of law, the case will be listed before the full EAT.

Generally the EAT will not allow points to be taken on appeal which were not raised at the Tribunal. New evidence will be admitted only if some reasonable explanation can be produced for its not having been put before the Tribunal and the new evidence is credible and would or might have had a decisive effect upon the decision.

Judgment

Judgment will be given orally immediately following the hearing or 'handed down' in written form on a day fixed later.

Legal aid

Legal aid is not available for representation at Tribunals. An Applicant may be eligible for limited assistance under the legal aid 'green form' scheme.

CHAPTER 10

Special Discrimination Rules

Individuals as Respondents

The way the discrimination rules operate in sex, race and disability discrimination claims allows individuals to bring complaints not only against the organisation but also against individuals within the organisation or associated with it who are responsible for the alleged acts of discrimination which form the substance of the complaint. This means that managers can actually be named as Respondents and the ET is entitled to conclude that both the organisation and the individuals were responsible for the discrimination alleged and to make separate awards against both groups for which the individuals in particular, are personally liable. In most cases the individuals named are senior managers within the organisation and the organisation will want to support the manager in his/her defence of the claim. However, there may be circumstances in which the two Respondents' (individual and employer) interests do not coincide:

- Where the company wants to argue that the manager did the act outside the course of employment, i.e., that no reasonable person would take the view that the acts alleged were part of the employment relationship. If a Tribunal accepts this defence the company will not be liable but this does not stop the named manager from being potentially liable.

- Alternatively, the company can accept that what was done was in the course of employment but argue that it has the benefit of the employer's statutory defence, i.e., that all such steps as were reasonably practicable were taken to prevent discrimination occurring – by the communication and implementation of anti-discrimination measures including but not limited to appropriate training. Again, if an employer is successful with this reasonably practicable defence this will result in the employer not being guilty of discrimination, although the ET may nevertheless make a finding and an award against the individual.

As a consequence where managers are jointly named as Respondents, it is always advisable to consider whether they should be separately represented. It is only where the primary defence is that the allegation of discrimination did not occur that the risk of conflict of interest does not arise.

The questionnaire procedure

Applicants claiming race, sex or disability discrimination can make use of the special questionnaire procedure. The questionnaires can be obtained from the Commission for Racial Equality, the Equal Opportunities Commission, Job Centres, Law Centres and Tribunals.

Questionnaires can be brought before or after a claim has been started in the ET and can be excellent tools to assist the Applicant in deciding whether to bring a complaint at all and, if so, what the nature of the complaint should be. Questionnaires can be used as evidence in the Employment Tribunal provided they comply with the necessary time limits.

- If no Tribunal application has yet been made, the questionnaire should be served within three months of the date of the act complained of.

- If an IT1 has been filed then the questionnaire should filed within 21 days of the filing of the IT1. If an Applicant misses these time limits then he/she can apply to the Employment Tribunal for leave to serve out of time. This also applies to questions which arise out of the Respondent's responses to the questionnaire.

There is no statutory time-frame within which the Respondent must reply to the questionnaire but it is advisable to attempt to reply within 21 days. If the Respondent fails to respond within a reasonable time-frame or provides evasive or uncommunicative responses, then the Tribunal may raise an adverse inference against that party. What that means is that the Tribunal may raise an inference that the Respondent was being deliberately evasive and uncooperative as a consequence of a desire to conceal a discriminatory act. The Respondent is then under an obligation to discharge this inference by demonstrating that there was some other reason for its behaviour.

Drafting the Questionnaire

A draft questionnaire is featured in Appendix 8.

The Applicant should first of all set out clearly to whom the questionnaire is addressed.

- At point 2 you should set out in as much detail as is relevant the background information upon which the claim is based. If your complaint is about a particular person or series of incidents, then you should set these out in as much detail as possible with dates, time, places and the names of those involved as well as any witnesses.

- Point 3 should set out why you believe that the behaviour to which you were subjected amounts to discrimination. If possible you should explain what type of discrimination you allege occurred (see chapter 1).

- At point 6 you should set out any questions you consider relevant. You should ask for information and not justification of actions (except in Disability Discrimination Act cases and indirect discrimination cases, in which case see below), e.g., the name of the decision-maker, factors on which the decision was based, etc.

- You are often trying to find out if there has been a difference in the treatment you were subjected to as opposed to other persons, so you will need to examine how the Respondent has behaved in other similar cases. For example, *'In the last two years, how many persons have been warned for non-attendance. Please break down these figures by [race/sex]'*

- You should also try and obtain details of why the Respondent thinks the cases should have been treated differently.

- In cases of indirect discrimination you should ask for details of how the Respondents justify the requirements imposed.

- Finally, you should ask general questions in relation to the kind of ethnic and/or gender monitoring the organisation carries out, what kind of equal opportunities and harassment procedures they have in place, requesting copies, the training of managers and employees in the implementation of the policies.

You should not ask for interpretation, e.g., 'what did he/she mean when he/she said ...?' nor should you hypothesise, e.g., 'what would have happened if ...?'.

In Disability Discrimination Act cases where a failure to make reasonable adjustments has been alleged, you should ensure that you ask what kind of adjustments were considered? By whom? And why they were rejected. If you suggested some adjustments whilst in employment or at interview you should ask why these were not adopted and who made the decision.

Finally, you should send the completed questionnaire to the Respondent. You do not need to send it to the ET.

The Respondent's reply

As soon as you receive the questionnaire you should immediately take steps to respond. If there is going to be any delay for whatever reason you should write immediately to the Applicant and explain. This will help you to argue that an inference of discrimination based on unreasonable delay should not be raised. You should immediately contact all relevant managers for the files on the individual and any relevant information.

You should attempt to answer each question as fully as possible but you should ensure that:

- You respect other employees' confidentiality so that you delete any names of other employees and replace these with codes, e.g., employee A, B, etc.

- Only answer questionnaires if they are clear and relevant. If you do not understand a question or its relevance, then you should ask for more details.

- If your monitoring and other systems are voluntary you should make this clear since otherwise the statistical evidence you provide may be distorted.

Turning to the questionnaire itself, a copy of which is in Appendix 8, at point 2 you will usually disagree with the series of events set out by the individual and will need to set out your own version of events. Again, do not include too much detail but ensure that if proceedings have already begun your response is consistent with the pleadings you have already submitted. At point 3b, if there is another reason why the treatment complained of was undertaken, then you should set this out.

At point 3a, you should complete this consistently with your answer to point 2. Often a simple statement 'because you were not treated unlawfully on grounds of your [disability/gender/ethnic origin]' will be enough. In indirect discrimination complaints your response will set out the justification for any requirement or condition imposed.

At 3c normally you will wish to respond ['not at all'].

You should copy your completed questionnaire and return a copy of it to the Applicant and/or his/her representative by registered post or recorded delivery. You do not need to send a copy of the completed questionnaire to the Employment Tribunal.

Disability Discrimination Act complaints

In broad terms DDA questionnaires and replies follow the same rules as above. However the major difference is at point 5. This point at section b asks for details of the justification for any treatment to which an individual was subjected. If replying to such questionnaires you should respond either by indicating that no less favourable treatment or failure to make reasonable adjustments has occurred. Alternatively, that if it has, the behaviour was justified. You will need to explain why.

Restricted reporting orders in sex and disability discrimination complaints

There are a number of restrictions the ET can place on the reporting and/or public access to information surrounding Employment Tribunals. The broad principle is that the Tribunal is a public forum, to which the public has full right of access at hearings and to any papers held in the public record (defence, origination application, etc). However, where the claims made involve allegations of sexual misconduct, the Tribunal can of its own volition, or on the application of either of the parties, make a restricted reporting order to prohibit the publication of any matter which would identify persons making and affected by allegations of sexual misconduct.

Persons in these circumstances are interpreted to cover only:

- victims

- alleged perpetrators

- witnesses directly affected by the allegations.

The Tribunal's discretion must be exercised sparingly and consideration must be given to the circumstances of each individual in respect of whom the order is granted. It is important to note only individuals can be protected in this way. Corporations and limited companies do not quality for this protection.

Where the pleadings disclose that an allegation of a sexual offence has been made, the Tribunal will of its own motion omit from and delete from any public documents any matters allowing an identification of the parties.

Disability Discrimination – a restricted reporting order can also be granted upon application by the Applicant only or by the Tribunal of its own motion where evidence of a personal nature will be given by the disabled Applicant.

Special equal value rules

For a general discussion as to the legal basis for equal pay complaints, see chapter 1. In broad terms, where a woman is arguing that she is being paid unequal pay whilst engaged on like work or work rated as equivalent in comparison to a man working for the same employer or an associated employer the normal Tribunal rules apply. Where, however, the allegation is that the work of the male comparator is of equal value, there are special Tribunal rules which deal with how claims are to be adjudicated upon. These are in addition to the ordinary Tribunal rules which unless inconsistent, also apply.

In equal value case the process is as follows:

1   First of all, the Tribunal must adjourn to invite the parties to attempt to settle the complaint. This is distinct from the provisions which require ACAS to attempt conciliation.

2   If no settlement is reached, then an initial hearing is convened at which the Tribunal considers whether the case is one in which there are no reasonable grounds for the determining that the work performed by the employee is of equal value. For example, if a job evaluation study has been undertaken which shows this. If the Tribunal believes the case has no real prospect of success, then it is not required to instruct an independent expert to carry out a job evaluation study. However, the Tribunal must allow the parties to make representations and to obtain their own expert's job evaluation study (should they so wish) before proceeding to strike out the complaint on this ground.

3   If the complaint proceeds, then the Tribunal may decide to assess whether the work is of equal value without the benefit of a report from an independent expert. Again, parties must be allowed to make representations before making a decision.

4   At this stage the Respondent may adduce evidence as to any genuine material factor which it alleges justifies the difference in pay and which is not related to the sex of the individual. If at this stage the Respondent is successful, then the complaint will fail. If, however, the Respondent is unsuccessful, then he/she cannot at a later date and after the question of equal value has been decided, raise the same defence. It is not possible to take two bites at the cherry in this respect.

5   The Tribunal may then proceed to appoint an independent expert to prepare a report. The Tribunal will instruct the expert to prepare the report indicating the names and addresses of the parties, the questions in issue and the name of the comparator as well as the addresses of the parties. Both of the parties receive a copy of the ET's commission.

The expert is asked to:

- Take account of all the information supplied and representations provided to him or her by the parties.

- Produce a written summary of the information and representations received, send this to the parties and invite comments.

- Report to the Tribunal in a document which sets out the above summary, the representations made and the conclusions drawn.

- Take no account of the difference of sex and at all times act fairly.

The job evaluation study must assess the value of the jobs by reference to objective factors such as skills, effort and responsibility and must not take into account any sexually discriminatory criteria. Note – it is the whole job which must be compared and not isolated aspects of it, e.g., management of others.

The Tribunal can impose a timetable on the expert and require that regular updates be given as to the progress of the report. If the report is to be delayed, then the expert must inform the Tribunal and explain any reasons for the delay. If either of the parties is at fault then the Tribunal can order that costs be awarded against that party and/or that the claim or defence be struck out. If the expert does not comply with the timetable set out for reasons unrelated to the conduct of the parties, then the Tribunal may either:

- insist that the expert comply with the required timetable

- provide the expert with a date later than the original date by which the report must be submitted

- replace the expert. However, before replacing an expert, the Tribunal must allow the parties to make representations.

Once the report has been received by the Tribunal it is provided to all the parties and the hearing will be reconvened. The parties may request that the expert attend the resumed hearing.

The Value of the report

The Tribunal does not have to accept the contents of the independent expert's report and it may exclude it entirely if:

- it believes that the expert did not follow the requirements set out earlier

- the conclusion contained in the report could not reasonably have been reached

- for some other reason the report is unsatisfactory (other than simple disagreement with the conclusion).

The parties may commission their own experts in order to make representations that the report should not be accepted on one of the above grounds and to provide an alternative interpretation of the conclusions. Note – the facts upon which the report is based cannot be attacked unless the expert reached no conclusion because of a refusal of a person to furnish information or documents.

The Tribunal makes a decision as to equal value and is not bound to accept the conclusions in the expert's report. If the Tribunal accepts that the work is of equal value and the Respondent has not already given evidence in relation to the genuine material factor which he/she alleges justifies the pay differential on grounds other than sex then he or she may now do so.

The Tribunal must give full written reasons for its decision.

Medical reports in discrimination complaints

Medical reports

In many different types of complaints medical reports will be of assistance, particularly in calculating losses to which an employee is entitled. In discrimination complaints in particular medical evidence may be required in two categories of claims:

1   Where it is alleged that the discrimination suffered has resulted in a personal injury for which the individual should be compensated (known as the *Sheriff v. Klyne Tugs* argument).

2   Where the parties are in dispute as to whether an individual is disabled for the purposes of the Disability Discrimination Act 1995.

Sheriff v. Klyne (Tugs) Argument

In the case of *Sheriff v. Klyne (Tugs) Limited* [1999], the Court of Appeal determined that compensation can be awarded by the Tribunal for personal injury which is caused by racial or other discrimination. This is particularly significant because mental injury suffered as a consequence of the discriminatory act does not have to be foreseeable, it just has to be caused by the discriminatory act. Medical evidence may therefore be used to demonstrate that mental injury has been suffered as a consequence of the discriminatory behaviour and an award of compensation can be made to compensate the Applicant for the fact that the injury is additional to the normal awards for injury to feelings and to compensate for loss of earnings (for further details of these, see chapter 8) normally awarded.

Disability

In Disability Discrimination Act 1995 complaints the parties may often dispute that the Applicant satisfies the test of disability in that he or she has:

> *A physical or mental impairment which has a substantial and long-term effect on the ability of the individual to carry out normal day-to-day activities.*

Medical evidence may be useful to establish whether the Applicant suffers from a well-recognised physical or mental impairment, when he/she began to suffer from this impairment and what effect it would have on his/her ability to carry out normal day-to-day activities as listed (see chapter 1). Whether or not the Applicant truly suffers a disability for these purposes will be determined by the Employment Tribunal and not by the medical evidence. However, evidence of this nature is useful to assist the Tribunal in coming to its decision.

Instructing medical experts

Applicants may wish to instruct medical experts to support their case and Respondents may wish to use medical evidence to dispute cases. Whichever party seeks medical evidence the following are useful pointers.

- Try to agree the fee up front.

- Note that the medical expert will reflect the content of his or her instructions in the report made. You should ensure that your letter of instruction is not too biased.

- It is useful for the expert to have all of the Applicant's medical records. If you are the Respondent, you should try and obtain these from the Applicant who will be able to get them from his or her doctor. If the Applicant feels uncomfortable about providing the Respondent with the medical records these can be provided directly to the medical expert.

- Ideally, the expert should examine the Applicant but note the Tribunal does not have the power to compel the Applicant to attend the medical examination. However, the Respondent will of course draw any refusal to the attention of the Tribunal in relation to the credibility of the Applicant.

- It is advisable to set out in a list of numbered questions the specific queries you wish answered, e.g., does the Applicant suffer from a physical or mental impairment? If so what is it? When did it first appear (in appropriate cases)? What was the cause?

Some Tribunals have taken to ordering parties to obtain joint medical reports which can then be agreed. In the writer's opinion this is an unhelpful process which can only serve to create delay whilst the parties argue over instructions to experts and the wording of the same.

Costs

Reasonable costs can be recovered from the ET for the attendance of a medical expert or for the provision of medical reports where these are 'essential' to the case. There is no maximum rate but the recommended rate varies between £58.50 and £116.50 an hour depending on status ranging from a junior hospital doctor to a senior consultant. GPs are normally paid in the middle of the range. Details of how much can be recovered can be obtained from the Employment Tribunal.

It is worth remembering that medical reports can be obtained but are only exchanged where the parties intend to rely upon them. If, therefore, a medical report is obtained which is unfavourable to either party's case, then, provided the parties do not intend to rely upon it, it does not need to be disclosed.

Matters where Tribunal Chairperson can sit alone

1. **TRADE UNION AND LABOUR RELATIONS (CONSOLIDATION) ACT 1992**	• S68 A: unauthorised deduction of union subscriptions • S192: claim for remuneration under protective award • SS161, 165 & 166: interim relief in cases involving dismissal on the ground of trade union membership and activities
2. **PENSION SCHEMES ACT 1993**	• S126: complaints to Employment Tribunal under the Act
3. **EMPLOYMENT RIGHTS ACT 1996**	**References Under ERA** • S11: written agreement of particulars of employment or itemised pay statement • S163: redundancy payments • S170: employer's payment **Complaints Under ERA** • S23: unauthorised deductions from wages • S34: guaranteed payments • S70(1): remuneration on suspension relating on medical grounds to claims under S 64 • S188: insolvency rights • SS128 131 & 132: interim relief in cases involving the dismissal of a health and safety representative, an occupational pension trustee, or an employee representative

	Appointments Under ERA • S206(4): appointment of a person to institute or continue proceedings on behalf of the estate of a deceased employee **Other** • S3: breach of contract
4. **TRANSFER OF UNDERTAKINGS (PROTECTION OF EMPLOYMENT) REGULATIONS 1981**	• Reg 11(5): compensation for failure to consult
5. **NATIONAL MINIMUM WAGE ACT 1998**	**Complaints** • S11: failure to keep records **Appeals** • S19: enforcement notices • S22: penalty notices
6. **PROCEEDINGS IN WHICH THE PARTIES HAVE CONSENTED IN WRITING TO THE CHAIRPERSON HEARING THE CASE ALONE**	
7. **PROCEEDINGS IN WHICH THE RESPONDENT DOES NOT CONTEST THE CASE**	

Claims and Remedies

CLAIMS	REMEDIES
(A) CONTRACT OF EMPLOYMENT	
1. **Breach of restrictive covenant**	• damages • interlocutory injunction
2. **Breach of contract**	• damages • if breach serious enough to be considered a repudiation of the contract, employee can treat himself/herself as discharged from his/her obligations under the contract
3. **Working Time**	
3.1 Complaints relating to employer's failure to permit exercise of rights in respect of working time or failure to give paid annual leave	• worker may present claim to Employment Tribunal
3.2 Victimisation – complaint that an employer has deliberately subjected a worker to any detriment on the ground that the worker has insisted, or proposed to insist, upon the observance of the Working Time Regulations	• declaration • money compensation
4. **Sunday Working**	
4.1 A complaint by a protected shop or betting worker or one who has opted out, that they have been subjected to a detriment by their employer on grounds of their refusal to work on a Sunday	• award of compensation – 'just and equitable'

4.2	Automatic unfair dismissal (if the reason or principal reason was the employee's refusal or proposal to refuse to work on Sunday)	• see 'normal' unfair dismissal claim • reinstatement • re-engagement • basic and additional compensation
5.	**Minimum notice of termination: failure to give due statutory notice**	• breach of contract • claim for damages
6.	**Failure of employer to provide employee with a written statement giving particulars of the major terms of employee's employment within two months of commencement of employment and/or failure to have the statements updated as and when there were changes to those terms**	• specification which particulars ought to have been given – those particulars are then deemed to have been given by employer • affirmation, amendment or replacement of incorrect particulars – the employer is then deemed to have given the corrected version
(B) PAY/PENSIONS		
1.	Unlawful deductions from wages	• order for repayment
2.	Unpaid contributions to occupational pension schemes	• order for repayment of contributions
(C) VICTIMISATION		
1.	Complaint relating to detriment in health and safety cases	• declaration • money compensation
2.	Complaint relating to detriment suffered on the grounds that the employee has refused or proposed to refuse to work on Sundays	• declaration • money compensation
3.	Complaint that an employer had deliberately subjected a worker to any detriment on the ground that the worker has insisted, or proposed to insist, upon the observance of the Working Time Regulations	• declaration • money compensation

4.	Complaint that an employer has subjected an employee to detriment on the ground that the employee has performed or proposed to perform any function of a trustee of an occupational pension scheme	• declaration • money compensation
5.	Complaint that an employer has deliberately subjected an employee to detriment on the ground that the employee has performed or proposed to perform any function as an employee representative under the Transfer of Undertakings (Protection of Employment) Regulations 1981 or the Trade Union and Labour Relations Consolidation Act 1992 or as a candidate for election as such a representative	• declaration • money compensation
6.	Complaint that an employer has deliberately subjected an employee to detriment on the ground that the employee has exercised or proposed to exercise his/her right to time off as a young employee or has claimed pay for time off which has been taken	• declaration • money compensation
7.	Complaint of victimisation by a worker for making a 'protected disclosure'	• declaration • money compensation
8.	Complaint of victimisation in relation to National Minimum Wage	• declaration • money compensation
9.	Complaint of victimisation by employee against employer in relation to tax credits	• declaration • money compensation

10. Complaint that an employer has by an act or deliberate failure to act subjected a worker to detriment in relation to the right to be accompanied by a trade union official/fellow worker at a disciplinary or grievance hearing	• declaration • money compensation
(D) TIME OFF FOR WORK	
1. Complaint of refusal by employer to allow time off work for public duties	• declaration • compensation
2. Redundancy: refusal to allow employee paid time off work to look for another job or to make arrangements for retraining	• declaration • order for payment
3. Employee representatives: refusal to allow time off to employee representatives to perform functions	• declaration • order for payment
(E) UNFAIR DISMISSAL	

1. Unfair dismissal	• reinstatement
	
	• re-engagement
	
	• compensation:
	  (1) Basic Award
	  (2) Compensatory Award to a maximum of £50,000 where the effective date of termination (EDT) occurred on or after 25 October 1999 (remains at £12,000 if EDT occurred on or after 1 April 1998 and before 25 October 1999)

(F) REDUNDANCY	
1. Redundancy – employer's breach of statutory duties to inform and consult	• declaration of default • Protective award calculated on 90 days maximum
(G) TRANSFER OF UNDERTAKINGS	
1. Failure to consult	• declaration • compensation
(H) MATERNITY & PARENTAL RIGHTS	
1. Infringement of employee's rights to return to work after maternity leave	• compensation (by way of unfair dismissal or redundancy payment) • reinstatement • re-engagement
2. Suspension from work on maternity grounds 2.1 Failure to provide alternative employment 2.2 Failure to pay remuneration during period of suspension	• compensation • order for payment
(I) EQUAL PAY	
1. Breach of provisions of Equal Pay Act 1970	• order for arrears • damages • declaration • injunction

(J) EQUAL OPPORTUNITIES	
1. Breach of provisions of Sex Discrimination Act 1975	• declaration of right • order for money compensation • a recommendation as to what steps the Respondent should take to obviate or reduce the adverse effect of the discrimination on the complainant
2. Breach of provisions of Race Relations Act 1976	• declaration of right • order for money compensation within limits • a recommendation as to what steps the Respondent should take to obviate or reduce the adverse effect of the discrimination on the complainant
3. Breach of provisions of Disability Discrimination Act 1995	• a declaration as to the rights of the complainant and the Respondent in relation to the matters to which the complaint relates • an order that the Respondent pays compensation to the complainant • a recommendation that the Respondent takes, within a specified period, action which appears to the Tribunal to be reasonable in all the circumstances of the case, for the purpose of obviating or reducing the adverse effect on the complainant of any matter to which the complaint arises

(K) TRADE UNIONS	
1. Breach of right to join trade union	• declaration (first stage) • compensation (second stage)
2. Complaint by trade union members of infringement of right not to be unjustifiably disciplined	• declaration • compensation • reimbursement
3. Complaint by trade union members in relation to unauthorised or excessive trade trade union subscription from wages	• declaration • order for refund
(L) LABOUR RELATIONS	
1. Complaint of unlawful refusal of employment on grounds related to trade union membership	• declaration • money compensation • recommendation that the employer within a specified time limit take action to obviate the effect of the unlawful refusal
2. Complaint of unlawful refusal of service of employment agency on grounds related to trade union membership	• declaration • money compensation • recommendation that the employer within a specified time limit take action to obviate the effect of the unlawful refusal
3. Unfair dismissal on Union grounds	• interim relief (preserves status quo before trial) • basic award • reinstatement • re-engagement

		• if order for reinstatement made but not carried out employee may qualify for a special award
4.	Victimisation: complaint by worker in respect of trade union recognition	• declaration • compensation
5.	Complaint by trade union officials relating to refusal of time off for trade union duties or refusal of payment in relation to time off taken	• declaration • money compensation • payment of sum due
6.	Complaint by trade union members relating to refusal of time off for trade union activities	• declaration • money compensation
7.	Complaint by trade union officials relating to refusal of time off to carry out health and safety duties	• declaration • money compensation
8.	Unfair dismissal on health and safety grounds	• interim relief • money award: basic, compensatory and special • reinstatement • re-engagement
9.	Victimisation on health and safety grounds	• declaration • money compensation
10.	Complaint of detriment relating to trade union activity	• declaration • money compensation
11.	Unfair dismissal relating to trade union activity	• interim relief • money award: basic, compensatory and special • reinstatement • re-engagement

Time limits for claims

STATUTE AND NATURE OF COMPLAINT	TIME LIMIT
1. **Equal Pay Act 1970**	
Breach of equality clause	six months from termination of employment (s 2(4))
2. **Sex Discrimination Act 1975**	
(a) act of sex discrimination	three months beginning with date of act (s 76(1))
(b) appeal against non-discrimination notice	six weeks from service of notice (s 68(1))
(c) complaint by Equal Opportunities Commission under s 73(1) (preliminary action before application to county court)	six months beginning with date of act complained of (s 76(4))
(d) application by Equal Opportunities Commission under s 72(3)(a) (enforcement of provisions relating to discriminatory advertisements, instructions and pressure to discriminate)	six months beginning with date of act complained of (s 76(3), as amended by the RRA s 79(4) Sch 4)
3. **Sex Discrimination Act 1986**	
(a) complaint of invalidity of discriminatory terms and rules	no time limit specified
(b) invalidity of discriminatory terms and rules under the Sex Discrimination Act 1986 s6(4A)	no limitation

4.	**Race Relations Act 1976**	
	(a) act of racial discrimination	three months beginning with date of act (s 68(1))
	(b) appeal against non-discrimination notice	six weeks from service of notice (s 59(1))
	(c) application by Commission for Racial Equality under s 63(2)(a)(enforcement of provisions relating to discriminatory advertisements, instructions and pressure to discriminate)	six months beginning with date of act (s 68(4))
	(d) complaint by Commission for Racial Equality under S64(1)(preliminary action before application to county court)	six months beginning with date of act (s 68(5))
5.	**Disability Discrimination Act 1995**	
	Act of disability discrimination	three months beginning with date of act complained of (Sch 3 para 3)
6.	**Employment Rights Act 1996**	
	(a) written statement of terms of employment	three months beginning with date on which employment ceased (s 11(4))
	(b) itemised pay statement	three months beginning with date on which employment ceased (s 11(4))
	(c) unauthorised deductions from wages	three months beginning with date of payment of wages from which deduction was made or date when payment received by employer (s 23(2),(4))
	(d) guarantee payments	three months beginning with date when payment was payable

(e) detriment relating to health and safety, Sunday working, working time, protected disclosure, duties of occupational pension trustee, functions of employee representative, leave for family or domestic reasons	three months beginning with date of act or failure (S 48(3))
(f) time off for public duties	three months from date of employer's failure to allow time off (s 51(2))
(g) time off for employee to look for work, etc.	three months beginning with date when time off should have been allowed (s 57(2))
(h) time off for antenatal care	three months beginning with date of appointment (s 57(2))
(i) time off for dependants	three months beginning with date when failure occurred (s 57B(2))
(j) time off for pension scheme trustees	three months beginning with date of employer's failure to allow time off (s 60(2))
(k) time off for employee representative	three months beginning with date when time off should have been allowed or day taken off (s 63(2))
(l) time off for young persons for study or training and right to remuneration	three months beginning with date when time off was taken or should have been allowed (s 63C(2))
(m) suspension from work on medical, or maternity, grounds	three months beginning with first day of suspension (s 70(2))
(n) parental leave	three months beginning with date of matters complained of (s 80(2))
(o) written statement of reasons for dismissal	three months beginning with effective date of termination of employment (s 93(3))
(p) unfair dismissal	three months beginning with effective date of termination of employment (s 111(2))
(q) interim relief	seven days immediately following the effective date of termination of employment (s 128))

(r)	redundancy payment	six months beginning with relevant date (s 164(1),(2))
(s)	insolvent employer: claims against Secretary of State (redundancy payment)	no time limit specified
(t)	payments equivalent to redundancy payments to civil servants, etc.	no time limit specified
(u)	insolvent employer: claims against Secretary of State (employer's debts)	three months beginning with date of communication of Secretary of State's decision (s 188(2))
(v)	S177 claims for payments equivalent to redundancy payments in respect of public sector employees	claims subject to six year period under the Limitation Act 1980 for actions founded on simple contract
7.	**Employment Relations Act 1999**	
	failure or threat to fail to comply with right to be accompanied at a disciplinary or grievance hearing	three months beginning with date of failure or threat (s 11(2))
8.	**Transfer of Undertakings (Protection of Employment) Regulations 1981 SI 1981/1794**	
	(a) failure to inform or consult	three months beginning with date of completion of transfer (reg 11 (8)(b))
	(b) claim by employee for compensation where order made by Tribunal under reg 11(4)	three months beginning with date of tribunal's order (reg 11 (8)(b))
9.	**Trade Union and Labour Relations Consolidation Act 1992**	
	(a) unjustifiable disciplining of trade union members	three months beginning with date of infringement (s 66(2))
	(b) application for compensation where Tribunal has made declaration of unjustifiable disciplining of trade union members	not earlier than four weeks beginning with date of declaration nor later than six months beginning with that date (s 67(3))

(c)	unauthorised deduction of union subscriptions	three months beginning with date of deduction (s 68A(1))
(d)	failure to comply with collective bargaining obligations regarding training	three months beginning with date of failure (s 70C(2))
(e)	wrongful deduction of political fund contributions or refusal to deduct union dues	three months beginning with date of payment of emoluments (s 87(2))
(f)	employer's failure to comply with order under s 87(5)	not earlier than four weeks beginning with date of order nor later than six months beginning with that date (s 87(6))
(g)	secret ballots on employer's premises	three months beginning with date of failure to comply (s 116(5))
(h)	refusal of employment on grounds of trade union membership	three months beginning with date of conduct complained of (s 139(1))
(i)	refusal of service of employment agency on grounds of trade union membership	three months beginning with date of conduct complained of (s 139(1))
(j)	trade union membership and activities (detriment short of dismissal)	three months beginning with date of last act or failure (s 147)
(k)	interim relief pending determination of complaint of unfair dismissal	seven days immediately following the effective date of termination (s 161(2))
(l)	time off for trade union duties and activities	three months from date of employer's failure to give time off or pay compensation (s 171)
(m)	exclusion or expulsion from trade union	six months beginning with date of refusal or expulsion (s 175)
(n)	application for compensation where Tribunal has made declaration of exclusion or expulsion from trade union	not earlier than four weeks beginning with date of declaration nor later than six months beginning with that date (s 176(3))
(o)	failure to consult in respect of redundancies	three months beginning with date on which dismissal takes effect (s 189(5))

(p) claim for remuneration under protective award	three months beginning with date of failure to pay (s 192(2))
(q) unfair dismissal under s 238 (failure to offer re-engagement where dismissal connected with lock-out, strike or other industrial action)	six months beginning with complainant's date of dismissal (s 239(2))
(r) detriment short of dismissal relating to collective bargaining rights	three months beginning with date of act or failure (Sch A1 para 157(1))
10. Pension Schemes Act 1993 insolvent employer: unpaid contributions to occupational pension scheme	three months beginning with date of communication of Secretary of State's decision (s 126(2))
11. Working Time Regulations 1998 S1 1998/1833 refusal to permit exercise of rights or failure to make payments in respect of annual leave	three months beginning with date when exercise of right should have been permitted or date when payment was payable (or six months in case of complaint by member of Armed Forces) reg 30(2))
12. National Minimum Wage Act 1998 (a) failure to allow access to records	three months following end of 14 days from receipt of production notice (s 11(3),(4))
(b) detriment relating to enforcement of rights, etc.	three months beginning with date of act or failure (s 24(2); ERA s 48(3))
(c) appeal against enforcement notice	four weeks following date of service of notice (s 19(4))
(d) appeal against penalty notice	four weeks following date of service of notice (s 22(1))
13. Health and Safety (Consultation with Employees) Regulations 1996 S1 1996/1513 failure to allow time off for employee safety representatives and candidates	three months from the date when the failure occurred (Sch 2 para 3)

14. **Employment Tribunals Extension of Jurisdiction (England and Wales) Order 1994 SI 1994/1623**	
(a) employee's contract claim	three months beginning with effective date of termination of employment or last working day (art 7)
(b) employer's contract claim	six weeks beginning with date of receipt of employee's claim (art 8)

Application to an Employment Tribunal

For office use

Received at ET

Case Number

Code

Initials

- If you fax this form you do not need to send one in the post.
- This form has to be photocopied. Please use CAPITALS and black ink (if possible).
- Where there are tick boxes, please tick the one that applies.

1 Please give the type of complaint you want the tribunal to decide (for example, unfair dismissal, equal pay). A full list is available from the tribunal office. If you have more than one complaint list them all.

4 Please give the dates of your employment

From _____ to _____

2 Please give your details

Mr ☐   Mrs ☐   Miss ☐   Ms ☐   Other _____

First names

Surname

Date of birth

Address

Postcode

Phone number

Daytime phone number

Please give an address to which we should send documents if different from above

Postcode

5 Please give the name and address of the employer, other organisation or person against whom this complaint is being brought

Name

Address

Postcode

Phone number

Please give the place where you worked or applied to work if different from above

Address

Postcode

3 If a representative is acting for you please give details (all correspondence will be sent to your representative)

Name

Address

Postcode

Phone

Fax

Reference

6 Please say what job you did for the employer (or what job you applied for). If this does not apply, please say what your connection was with the employer

7 Please give the number of normal basic hours worked
   each week

   Hours per week

9 If your complaint is not about dismissal, please give
   the date when the matter you are complaining about
   took place

8 Please give your earning details

   Basic wage or salary

   £   :   per

   Average take home pay

   £   :   per

   Other bonuses or benefits

   £   :   per

10 Unfair dismissal applicants only

   Please indicate what you are seeking at this stage, if you
   win your case

   ☐ Reinstatement: to carry on working in your old job as
       before (an order for reinstatement normally includes
       an award of compensation for loss of earnings).

   ☐ Re-engagement: to start another job or new contract
       with your old employer (an order for re-engagement
       normally includes an award of compensation for loss
       of earnings).

   ☐ Compensation only: to get an award of money

11 Please give details of your complaint

   If there is not enough space for your answer, please continue on a separate sheet and attach it to this form.

12 Please sign and date this form, then send it to the address on the back page of the booklet *How to apply to an Employment
   Tribunal* (URN 99/613), available from the DTI on 0870 150 2500

   Signed   Date

IT1(E/W)

APPENDIX 5

EMPLOYMENT TRIBUNALS
NOTICE OF APPEARANCE BY RESPONDENT

In the application of

Case Number
(please quote in all correspondence)

* This form has to be photocopied, if possible please use Black Ink and Capital letters
* If there is not enough space for your answer, please continue on a separate sheet and attach it to this form

1. Full name and address of the Respondent:	3. Do you intend to resist the application? (Tick appropriate box)
	YES ☐ NO ☐
	4. Was the applicant dismissed? (Tick appropriate box)
	YES ☐ Please give reason below NO ☐
	Reason for dismissal:
	5. Are the dates of employment given by the applicant correct? (Tick appropriate box)
	YES ☐ NO ☐ please give correct dates
Post Code:	Began on
Telephone number:	Ended on
2. If you require documents and notices to be sent to a representative or any other address in the United Kingdom please give details:	6. Are the details given by the applicant about wages/salary, take home or other bonuses correct? (Tick appropriate box)
	YES ☐ NO ☐ Please give correct details below
	Basic Wages/Salary £ per
	Average Take Home Pay £ per
	Other Bonuses/Benefits £ per
	PLEASE TURN OVER
Post Code:	for office use only
Reference:	Date of receipt Initials
Telephone number:	

Form IT3 E&W - 9/98

7. Give particulars of the grounds on which you intend to resist the application.

8. Please sign and date the form.

Signed   Dated

DATA PROTECTION ACT 1984
We may put some of the information you give on this form on to a computer. This helps us to monitor progress and produce statistics. We may also give information to:
* the other party in the case
* other parts of the DTI and organisations such as ACAS (Advisory Conciliation and Arbitration Service), the Equal Opportunities Commission or the Commission for Racial Equality.

Please post or fax this form to : The Regional Secretary

*IF YOU FAX THE FORM, DO NOT POST A COPY AS WELL
*IF YOU POST THE FORM, TAKE A COPY FOR YOUR RECORDS

Form IT3 E&W - 9/98

Laserform International 7/99

STATUTORY INSTRUMENTS

1993 No. 2687

INDUSTRIAL TRIBUNALS

The Industrial Tribunals (Constitution and Rules of Procedure) Regulations 1993

Made - - - -	*17th November 1993*	
Laid before Parliament	*24th November 1993*	
Coming into force	*16th December 1993*	

LONDON:HMSO

1993 No. 2687

INDUSTRIAL TRIBUNALS

The Industrial Tribunals (Constitution and Rules of Procedure) Regulations 1993

Made - - - -	*17th November 1993*
Laid before Parliament	*24th November 1993*
Coming into force	*16th December 1993*

ARRANGEMENT OF REGULATIONS AND RULES

5. Time and place of hearing.

6. Entitlement to bring or contest proceedings.

7. Pre-hearing review.

8. The hearing.

9. Procedure at hearing.

10. Decision of tribunal.

11. Review of tribunal's decision.

12. Costs.

13. Miscellaneous powers.

14. Restricted reporting orders.

15. Extension of time.

16. Directions.

17. Joinder and representative respondents.

18. Combined proceedings.

19. Transfer of proceedings.

20. Notices, etc.

SCHEDULE 2 — THE INDUSTRIAL TRIBUNALS COMPLEMENTARY RULES OF PROCEDURE

For use only in proceedings involving an equal value claim.

4. Power to require further particulars and attendance of witnesses and to grant discovery.

8A. Procedure relating to expert's report.

9. Procedure at hearing.

10. Decision of tribunal.

12. Costs.

13. Miscellaneous powers.

20. Notices, etc.

SCHEDULE 3 — THE INDUSTRIAL TRIBUNALS (LEVY APPEALS) RULES OF PROCEDURE

For use only in proceedings in levy appeals.

1. Notice of appeal.

2. Action upon receipt of appeal.

3. Further particulars of appeal.

4. Withdrawal of appeal or assessment.

5. Entry of appeal.

6. Directions for further particulars.

7. Attendance of witnesses and discovery.

8. Time and place of hearing of appeal.

2

SCHEDULE 4 — THE INDUSTRIAL TRIBUNALS (IMPROVEMENT AND PROHIBITION NOTICES APPEALS) RULES OF PROCEDURE

For use only in proceedings on an appeal against an improvement or prohibition notice.

SCHEDULE 5 — THE INDUSTRIAL TRIBUNALS (NON-DISCRIMINATION NOTICES APPEALS) RULES OF PROCEDURE

For use only in proceedings on an appeal against a non-discrimination notice.

3

9. Review of tribunal's decision.

10. Costs.

11. Miscellaneous powers.

12. Restricted reporting orders.

13. Notices, etc.

The Secretary of State, in exercise of the powers conferred on him by section 24(2) of the Health and Safety at Work etc. Act 1974(**a**), section 128(1) and (5), section 154(3) and paragraphs 1, 1A and 1B of Schedule 9 to the Employment Protection (Consolidation) Act 1978(**b**), and of all other powers enabling him in that behalf, and after consultation with the Council on Tribunals, hereby makes the following Regulations:–

Citation, commencement and revocation

1.—(1) These Regulations may be cited as the Industrial Tribunals (Constitution and Procedure) Regulations 1993 and the Rules of Procedure contained in Schedules 1, 2, 3, 4 and 5 to these Regulations may be referred to, respectively, as–

(a) the Industrial Tribunals Rules of Procedure 1993;

(b) the Industrial Tribunals Complementary Rules of Procedure 1993;

(c) the Industrial Tribunals (Levy Appeals) Rules of Procedure 1993;

(d) the Industrial Tribunals (Improvement and Prohibition Notices Appeals) Rules of Procedure 1993; and

(e) the Industrial Tribunals (Non-Discrimination Notices Appeals) Rules of Procedure 1993.

(2) These Regulations shall come into force on 16th December 1993.

(3) The following Regulations are hereby revoked–

The Industrial Tribunals (England and Wales) Regulations 1965(**c**)

The Industrial Tribunals (England and Wales) (Amendment) Regulations 1967(**d**)

The Industrial Tribunals (England and Wales) (Amendment) Regulations 1970(**e**)

The Industrial Tribunals (Improvement and Prohibition Notices Appeals) Regulations 1974(**f**)

The Industrial Tribunals (Amendment) Regulations 1977(**g**)

The Industrial Tribunals (Non-Discrimination Notices Appeals) Regulations 1977(**h**)

The Industrial Tribunals (Rules of Procedure) Regulations 1985(**i**) .

Interpretation

2.—(1) In these Regulations and in Schedules 1, 2, 3, 4 and 5, unless the context otherwise requires–

"the 1978 Act" means the Employment Protection (Consolidation) Act 1978;

"the 1992 Act" means the Trade Union and Labour Relations (Consolidation) Act 1992(**j**);

(**a**) 1974 c.37.
(**b**) 1978 c.44; section 128 was amended by the Employment Act 1980 (c.42) (the 1980 Act), Schedule 1, paragraph 16, by the Criminal Justice Act 1982 (c.48), sections 37, 38 and 46 and by the Trade Union Reform and Employment Rights Act 1993 (c.19) (the 1993 Act), section 36 and Schedule 10. Paragraph 1 of Schedule 9 was amended by the 1980 Act, Schedule 1, paragraph 26; by the Equal Pay (Amendment) Regulations 1983 (S.I. 1983/1794), regulation 3; by the Employment Act 1989 (c.38), Schedule 6, paragraph 26 and by the 1993 Act, section 40 and Schedule 8, paragraph 28(a). Section 1A was inserted by the Employment Act 1989, section 20 and was amended by the 1993 Act, Schedule 8, paragraph 28(b). Paragraph 1B was inserted by the 1993 Act, Schedule 8, paragraph 28(c).
(**c**) S.I. 1965/1101, amended by S.I. 1967/301, S.I. 1970/941 and by the Courts and Legal Services Act 1990 (c.41), Schedule 10, paragraph 27.
(**d**) S.I. 1967/301.
(**e**) S.I. 1970/941.
(**f**) S.I. 1974/1925.
(**g**) S.I. 1977/1473.
(**h**) S.I. 1977/1094.
(**i**) S.I. 1985/16.
(**j**) 1992 c.52.

4

"chairman" means the President or a member of the panel of chairmen selected in accordance with regulation 7(1), or the President where a Minister of the Crown so directs in accordance with section 128(6) of the 1978 Act(a);

"the clerk" means the person appointed as clerk to the tribunal by the Secretary of the Tribunals or a Regional Secretary to act in that capacity at one or more hearings;

"hearing" means a sitting of a tribunal duly constituted for the purpose of receiving evidence, hearing addresses and witnesses or doing anything lawfully requisite to enable the tribunal to reach a decision on any question;

"the Office of the Tribunals" means the Central Office of the Industrial Tribunals (England and Wales);

"panel of chairmen" means the panel appointed under regulation 5(1)(a);

"the President" means the President of the Industrial Tribunals (England and Wales) or the person nominated by the Lord Chancellor to discharge for the time being the functions of the President;

"Regional Chairman" means a member of the panel of chairmen who has been appointed to the position of Regional Chairman in accordance with regulation 6 (1) or who has been nominated to discharge the functions of a Regional Chairman in accordance with regulation 6(2);

"Regional Office of the Industrial Tribunals" means a regional office which has been established under the Office of the Tribunals for an area specified by the President;

"Regional Secretary" means the person for the time being acting as the secretary of a Regional Office of the Industrial Tribunals;

"Register" means the Register of applications, appeals and decisions kept in pursuance of regulation 9;

"the Secretary" means the person for the time being appointed to act as the Secretary of the Office of the Tribunals;

"tribunal" means an industrial tribunal (England and Wales) established in pursuance of regulation 4 and in relation to any proceedings means the tribunal to which the proceedings have been referred by the President or a Regional Chairman.

(2) In these Regulations, in so far as they relate to the rules in Schedules 1 and 2, and in those Schedules, unless the context otherwise requires–

"the 1970 Act" means the Equal Pay Act 1970(b);

"the 1975 Act" means the Sex Discrimination Act 1975(c);

"the 1976 Act" means the Race Relations Act 1976(d);

"the 1986 Act" means the Sex Discrimination Act 1986(e);

"decision" in relation to a tribunal includes–

a declaration,

an order, including an order striking out any originating application or notice of appearance made under rule 4(7) or 13(2),

a recommendation or an award of the tribunal, and

a determination under rule 6,

but does not include any other interlocutory order or any other decision on an interlocutory matter;

"equal value claim" means a claim by an applicant which rests upon entitlement to the benefit of an equality clause by virtue of the operation of section 1(2)(c) of the Equal Pay Act;

"expert" means a member of the panel of independent experts within the meaning

---

(a) Section 128(6) was inserted into the Employment Protection (Consolidation) Act 1978 (c.44) by the Trade Union Reform and Employment Rights Act 1993 (c.19), section 36(3).

(b) 1970 c.41, which has been amended. The amendments relevant to these Regulations are as follows. Section 1 was amended by the Sex Discrimination Act 1975 (c.65) (the 1975 Act), section 8 and Schedule 1, Part I; by the Equal Pay (Amendment) Regulations 1983 (S.I. 1983/1794) (the 1983 Regulations); by the Armed Forces Act 1981 (c.55), section 28 and Schedule 5, paragraph 1; by the Contracts (Applicable Law) Act 1990 (c.36), section 5 and Schedule 4; by the Trade Union and Labour Relations (Consolidation) Act 1992 (c.52), Schedule 2, paragraph 3(1) and (2); and by the Trade Union Reform and Employment Rights Act 1993 (c.19), Schedule 7, paragraph 8. Section 2 was amended by the 1975 Act, section 8 and Schedule 1, Part I and by the Employment Protection (Consolidation) Act 1978 (c.44), section 159 and Schedule 17. Section 2A was inserted by the 1983 Regulations.

(c) 1975 c.65, to which there are amendments not relevant to these Regulations.

(d) 1976 c.74, to which there are amendments not relevant to these Regulations.

(e) 1986 c.59; for relevant amendments see below.

5

of section 2A(4) of the Equal Pay Act;

"report" means a report required by a tribunal to be prepared by an expert, pursuant to section 2A(1)(b) of the Equal Pay Act;

"respondent" means a party to the proceedings before a tribunal other than the applicant.

(3) In these Regulations, in so far as they relate to the rules in Schedule 3, and in that Schedule, unless the context otherwise requires–

"the 1982 Act" means the Industrial Training Act 1982(a);

"the Board" means in relation to an appeal the respondent industrial training board;

"levy" means a levy imposed under section 11 of the 1982 Act.

(4) In these Regulations, in so far as they relate to the rules in Schedule 4, and in that Schedule, unless the context otherwise requires–

"the 1974 Act" means the Health and Safety at Work etc. Act 1974;

"decision" in relation to a tribunal includes a direction under rule 4 and any order which is not an interlocutory order;

"improvement notice" means a notice under section 21 of the 1974 Act;

"inspector" means a person appointed under section 19(1) of the 1974 Act;

"prohibition notice" means a notice under section 22 of the 1974 Act;

"respondent" means the inspector who issued the improvement notice or prohibition notice which is the subject of the appeal.

(5) In these Regulations, in so far as they relate to the rules in Schedule 5, and in that Schedule, unless the context otherwise requires–

"the 1975 Act" means the Sex Discrimination Act 1975;

"the 1976 Act" means the Race Relations Act 1976;

"decision" in relation to a tribunal includes the direction under section 68(3) of the 1975 Act or, as the case may be, under section 59(3) of the 1976 Act and any other order which is not an interlocutory order;

"non-discrimination notice" means a notice under section 67 of the 1975 Act or, as the case may be, under section 58 of the 1976 Act;

"respondent" means the Equal Opportunities Commission established under section 53 of the 1975 Act or, as the case may be, the Commission for Racial Equality established under section 43 of the 1976 Act.

President of Industrial Tribunals

3.—(1) There shall be a President of the Industrial Tribunals (England and Wales) who shall be appointed by the Lord Chancellor and shall be a person having a seven year general qualification within the meaning of section 71 of the Courts and Legal Services Act 1990(b).

(2) The President may resign his office by notice in writing to the Lord Chancellor.

(3) The President shall vacate his office at the end of the completed year of service in the course of which he attains the age of 72 years.

(4) If the Lord Chancellor is satisfied that the President is incapacitated by infirmity of mind or body from discharging the duties of his office, or the President is adjudged to be bankrupt or makes a composition or arrangement with his creditors, the Lord Chancellor may revoke his appointment.

(5) The functions of President under these Regulations may, if he is for any reason unable to act or during any vacancy in his office, be discharged by a person nominated for that purpose by the Lord Chancellor.

Establishment of industrial tribunals

4.—(1) The President shall from time to time determine the number of tribunals to be established in England and Wales for the purposes of determining proceedings.

(2) The President or, in relation to the area specified in relation to him, a Regional

---

(a) 1982 c.10. (b) 1990 c.41.

Chairman shall determine at what times and in what places in England and Wales tribunals shall sit.

Panels of members of tribunals

5.—(1) There shall be three panels of members of the Industrial Tribunals (England and Wales), namely–

    (a) a panel of persons, having a seven year general qualification within the meaning of the Courts and Legal Services Act 1990, appointed by the Lord Chancellor;

    (b) a panel of persons appointed by the Secretary of State after consultation with such organisations or associations of organisations representative of employees as he sees fit; and

    (c) a panel of persons appointed by the Secretary of State after consultation with such organisations or associations of organisations representative of employers as he sees fit.

(2) Members of the panels constituted under these Regulations shall hold and vacate office under the terms of the instrument under which they are appointed but may resign their office by notice in writing, in the case of a member of the panel of chairmen, to the Lord Chancellor and, in any other case, to the Secretary of State; and any such member who ceases to hold office shall be eligible for reappointment.

Regional Chairmen

6.—(1) The President may from time to time appoint Regional Chairmen from the panel of chairmen and each Regional Chairman shall be responsible for the administration of justice by tribunals in the area specified by the President in relation to him.

(2) The President or the Regional Chairman for an area may from time to time nominate a member of the panel of chairmen to discharge for the time being the functions of the Regional Chairman for that area.

Composition of tribunals

7.—(1) For each hearing of any matter before a tribunal the President or the Regional Chairman shall, subject to paragraph 5, select a chairman, who shall be the President or a member of the panel of chairmen, and the President or the Regional Chairman may select himself.

(2) In any proceedings which are to be determined by a tribunal comprising a chairman (selected in accordance with paragraph (1) above) and two other members, those other members shall be selected by the President or by the Regional Chairman, as to one member from the panel of persons appointed by the Secretary of State under regulation 5(1)(b) and as to the other from the panel of persons appointed under regulation 5(1)(c).

(3) In any proceedings which are to be determined by a tribunal whose composition is described in paragraph (2), those proceedings may, with the consent of the parties, be heard and determined in the absence of any one member other than the chairman, and in that event the tribunal shall be properly constituted.

(4) The President or the Regional Chairman may at any time select from the appropriate panel another person in substitution for the chairman or other member of the tribunal previously selected to hear any proceedings before a tribunal.

(5) Paragraph (1) does not apply where a Minister of the Crown has issued a direction in accordance with section 128(6) of the 1978 Act (direction on grounds of national security that proceedings be heard and determined by the President).

Proceedings of tribunals

8.—(1) Subject to paragraphs (2), (3) and (4), the rules in Schedule 1 shall apply in relation to all proceedings before a tribunal except where separate rules of procedure made under the provisions of any enactment are applicable.

(2) In proceedings to which the rules in Schedule 1 apply and which involve an equal

7

value claim, the rules in Schedule 2 (including rule 8A) shall apply in place of rules 4, 9, 10, 12, 13 and 20 in Schedule 1.

(3) The rules contained in Schedules 1 and 2 shall apply in proceedings to which they relate where–

(a) the respondent or one of the respondents resides or carries on business in England and Wales; or

(b) had the remedy been by way of action in the county court, the cause of action would have arisen wholly or in part in England and Wales; or

(c) the proceedings are to determine a question which has been referred to the tribunal by a court in England or Wales.

(4) The rules in Schedules 3, 4 and 5 shall apply in relation to proceedings before a tribunal which relate to matters arising in England and Wales and consist, respectively, in–

(a) an appeal by a person assessed to levy imposed under a levy order made under section 12 of the 1982 Act(a);

(b) an appeal against an improvement or prohibition notice under section 23 of the 1974 Act; and

(c) an appeal against a non-discrimination notice under section 68 of the 1975 Act or section 59 of the 1976 Act.

Register

9. The Secretary shall maintain a Register of applications, appeals and decisions which shall be open to the inspection of any person without charge at all reasonable hours.

Proof of decisions of tribunals

10. The production in any proceedings in any court of a document purporting to be certified by the Secretary to be a true copy of an entry of a decision in the Register shall, unless the contrary is proved, be sufficient evidence of the document and of the facts stated therein.

Transitional provisions relating to rules of procedure

11.—(1) The rules in Schedules 1, 2, 3, 4 and 5 (in this regulation referred to as "the new rules") shall apply in all proceedings to which they relate, irrespective of when those proceedings were commenced, as from 16th December 1993, and the rules of procedure in–

(a) Schedule 2 to the Industrial Tribunals (England and Wales) Regulations 1965;

(b) the Schedule to the Industrial Tribunals (Improvement and Prohibition Notices Appeal) Regulations 1974;

(c) the Schedule to the Industrial Tribunals (Non-Discrimination Notices Appeals) Regulations 1977;

(d) the Industrial Tribunals Rules of Procedure 1985 ("the 1985 rules"); and

(e) the Industrial Tribunals Complementary Rules of Procedure 1985,

(in this regulation together referred to as "the old rules") shall cease to have effect in relation to proceedings on that date.

(2) Anything done validly under or pursuant to the old rules before 16th December 1993 shall be treated as having been done validly for the purposes of these Regulations and the new rules, whether or not what was done could have been done under or pursuant to these Regulations and the new rules.

(3) Notwithstanding paragraph (1), in any proceedings in which a pre-hearing assessment (under Rule 6 of the 1985 rules) has taken place or commenced before 16th December 1993, Rule 6 of those rules shall continue to have effect in relation to those proceedings and no pre-hearing review (under rule 7 in Schedule 1) may take place.

(4) Where the first fixing of the date of a pre-hearing assessment occurs before 16th

---

(a) Section 12 was amended by the Employment Act 1989 (c.38), Schedule 4, paragraph 11.

December 1993 but paragraph (3) does not apply, the hearing shall be refixed as a pre-hearing review (under rule 7 in Schedule 1).

Transitional provisions relating to composition of tribunals

12.—(1) Except as mentioned in paragraph (2), a tribunal hearing an originating application on or after 16th December 1993 shall be composed of a chairman and two other members (or, with the consent of the parties, a chairman and one other member) where the first fixing of a date for the hearing of the originating application occurred before 30th November 1993.

(2) A tribunal hearing such an originating application on or after 16th December 1993 may be composed of a chairman alone for either of the following purposes–

    (a) making an order dismissing the proceedings where the appellant or applicant has given written notice of the abandonment of the proceedings; and

    (b) deciding an application in accordance with the written agreement of the parties.

Signed by order of the Secretary of State

Ann Widdecombe
Parliamentary Under Secretary of State,
Department of Employment.

17th November 1993

RULES OF PROCEDURE

Originating application

1.—(1) Where proceedings are brought by an applicant, they shall be instituted by the applicant presenting to the Secretary an originating application, which shall be in writing and shall set out–

   (a) the name and address of the applicant and, if different, an address within the United Kingdom to which he requires notices and documents relating to the proceedings to be sent;

   (b) the names and addresses of the person or persons against whom relief is sought; and

   (c) the grounds, with particulars thereof, on which relief is sought.

(2) Where the Secretary is of the opinion that the originating application does not seek or on the facts stated therein cannot entitle the applicant to a relief which a tribunal has power to give, he may give notice to that effect to the applicant stating the reasons for his opinion and informing him that the application will not be registered unless he states in writing that he wishes to proceed with it.

(3) An application in respect of which such a notice has been given shall not be treated as having been received for the purpose of rule 2 unless the applicant intimates in writing to the Secretary that he wishes to proceed with it; and upon receipt of such an intimation the Secretary shall proceed in accordance with that rule.

(4) In the case of an originating application in respect of a complaint under section 6(4A) of the 1986 Act(a) relating to a term of a collective agreement, the following persons, whether or not identified in the originating application, shall be regarded as the persons against whom relief is sought and shall be treated as respondents for the purposes of these rules, that is to say–

   (a) the applicant's employer (or prospective employer), and

   (b) every organisation of employers and organisation of workers, and every association of or representative of such organisations, which, if the term were to be varied voluntarily, would be likely, in the opinion of the tribunal, to negotiate the variation;

provided that such an organisation or association shall not be treated as a respondent if the tribunal, having made such enquiries of the applicant and such other enquiries as it thinks fit, is of the opinion that it is not reasonably practicable to identify the organisation or association.

(5) Where proceedings are referred to a tribunal by a court, these rules shall be applied to them, except where the rules are inappropriate, as if the proceedings had been instituted by the presentation of an originating application.

Action upon receipt of originating application

2.—(1) Upon receiving an originating application the Secretary shall–

   (a) send a copy of it to the respondent;

   (b) give every party notice in writing of the case number of the application (which shall constitute the title of the proceedings) and of the address to which notices and other communications to the Secretary shall be sent; and

   (c) send to the respondent a notice in writing which includes information, as appropriate to the case, about the means and time for entering an appearance, the consequences of failure to do so, and the right to receive a copy of the decision.

(2) The Secretary shall, subject to rule 13(6), enter particulars of an originating application in the Register either within 28 days of receiving it or, if that is not practicable, as soon as reasonably practicable thereafter.

(3) The Secretary shall also, in all cases, notify the parties that in every case where an enactment provides for conciliation, the services of a conciliation officer are available to them.

Appearance by respondent

3.—(1) A respondent shall, within 14 days of receiving the copy of the originating application, enter an appearance to the proceedings by presenting to the Secretary a written notice of appearance–

   (a) setting out his full name and address and, if different, an address within the United Kingdom to which he requires notices and documents relating to the proceedings to be sent;

   (b) stating whether or not he intends to resist the application; and

---

(a) Section 6(4A) was inserted by the Trade Union Reform and Employment Rights Act 1993 (c.19), section 32.

(c) if he does intend to resist it, setting out sufficient particulars to show on what grounds.
Upon receipt of a notice of appearance the Secretary shall send a copy of it to each other party.

(2) A respondent who has not entered an appearance shall not be entitled to take any part in the proceedings except–

(a) to apply under rule 15 for an extension of the time appointed by this rule for entering an appearance;

(b) to make an application under rule 4(1)(a);

(c) to make an application under rule 11(4) in respect of rule 11(1)(b);

(d) to be called as a witness by another person;

(e) to be sent a copy of a document or corrected entry in pursuance of rule 10(5), 10(10) or 10(11);

and in the rules which follow, the word "party" only includes such a respondent in relation to his entitlement to take such a part in the proceedings, and in relation to any such part which he takes.

(3) A notice of appearance which is presented to the Secretary after the time appointed by this rule for entering appearances shall be deemed to include an application under rule 15(1) (by the respondent who presented the notice) for an extension of the time so appointed.

(4) Without prejudice to rule 15(3), if a chairman grants an application deemed to be included in a notice of appearance by paragraph (3) (which he may do notwithstanding that the grounds of the application are not stated) the Secretary shall send a copy of the notice of appearance to each other party.

(5) A chairman shall not refuse such an application unless he has sent notice to the person wishing to enter an appearance giving that person an opportunity to show cause why an extension should be granted.

Power to require further particulars and attendance of witnesses and to grant discovery

4.—(1) A tribunal may, on the application of a party made either by notice to the Secretary or at the hearing of the originating application, or of its own motion–

(a) require a party to furnish in writing to the person specified by the tribunal further particulars of the grounds on which that party relies and of any facts and contentions relevant thereto,

(b) require one party to grant to another such discovery or inspection (including the taking of copies) of documents as might be granted by a county court,

and may appoint the time at or within which and the place at which any act required in pursuance of this rule is to be done.

(2) A tribunal may, on the application of a party made either by notice to the Secretary or at the hearing of the originating application, or of its own motion–

(a) require the attendance of any person, including a party, as a witness, wherever such person may be within Great Britain, and

(b) if it does so require the attendance of a person, require him to produce any document relating to the matter to be determined,

and may appoint the time and place at which the person is to attend and, where appropriate, the time at or within which and the place at which any such document is to be produced.

(3) A tribunal may, on the application of a party made by notice to the Secretary or of its own motion, require a party in writing to furnish to the tribunal a written answer to any question if it considers–

(a) that the answer of the party to that question may help to clarify any issue likely to arise for determination in the proceedings, and

(b) that it would be likely to assist the progress of the proceedings for that answer to be available to the tribunal before the hearing,

and may appoint the time within which the written answer is to be furnished. Upon the imposition of such a requirement, the Secretary shall send a copy of the requirement to each other party; and he shall send a copy of the answer to each other party.

(4) The tribunal shall take account of a written answer furnished pursuant to paragraph (3) in the same way as it takes account of representations in writing presented by a party pursuant to rule 8(5).

(5) Where a requirement has been imposed under paragraph (1), (2) or (3)–

(a) on a party in his absence; or

(b) on a person other than a party,

11

that party or person may make an application to the tribunal to vary or set aside the requirement by notice to the Secretary given before the time at which or, as the case may be, the expiration of the time within which the requirement is to be complied with; and the Secretary shall give notice of the application to each party or, where applicable, to each party other than the party making the application.

(6) Every document containing a requirement imposed under paragraph (1)(b) or (2) shall contain a reference to the fact that, under paragraph 1(7) of Schedule 9 to the 1978 Act, any person who without reasonable excuse fails to comply with any such requirement shall be liable on summary conviction to a fine, and the document shall state the amount of the current maximum fine.

(7) If a requirement under paragraph (1) or (3) is not complied with, a tribunal, before or at the hearing, may strike out the whole or part of the originating application, or, as the case may be, of the notice of appearance, and, where appropriate, direct that a respondent shall be debarred from defending altogether: but a tribunal shall not so strike out or direct unless it has sent notice to the party who has not complied with the requirement giving him an opportunity to show cause why the tribunal should not do so.

Time and place of hearing

5.—(1) The President or a Regional Chairman shall fix the date, time and place of the hearing of the originating application and the Secretary shall send to each party a notice of hearing together with information and guidance as to attendance at the hearing, witnesses and the bringing of documents, representation by another person and the making of written representations.

(2) The Secretary shall send the notice of hearing to every party not less than 14 days before the date fixed for the hearing except–
- (a) where the Secretary has agreed a shorter time with the parties; or
- (b) on an application for interim relief made under section 77 of the 1978 Act or section 161 of the 1992 Act.

Entitlement to bring or contest the proceedings

6.—(1) A tribunal may at any time before the hearing of an originating application, on the application of a party made by notice to the Secretary or of its own motion, determine any issue relating to the entitlement of any party to bring or contest the proceedings to which the originating application relates.

(2) A tribunal shall not determine such an issue unless the Secretary has sent notice to each of the parties giving them an opportunity to submit representations in writing and to advance oral argument before the tribunal.

Pre-hearing review

7.—(1) A tribunal may at any time before the hearing of an originating application, on the application of a party made by notice to the Secretary or of its own motion, conduct a pre-hearing review, consisting of a consideration of--
- (a) the contents of the originating application and notice of appearance;
- (b) any representations in writing; and
- (c) any oral argument advanced by or on behalf of a party.

(2) If a party applies for a pre-hearing review and the tribunal determines that there shall be no review, the Secretary shall send notice of the determination to that party.

(3) A pre-hearing review shall not take place unless the Secretary has sent notice to the parties giving them an opportunity to submit representations in writing and to advance oral argument at the review if they so wish.

(4) If upon a pre-hearing review the tribunal considers that the contentions put forward by any party in relation to a matter required to be determined by a tribunal have no reasonable prospect of success, the tribunal may make an order against that party requiring the party to pay a deposit of an amount not exceeding £150 as a condition of being permitted to continue to take part in the proceedings relating to that matter.

(5) No order shall be made under this rule unless the tribunal has taken reasonable steps to ascertain the ability of the party against whom it is proposed to make the order to comply with such an order, and has taken account of any information so ascertained in determining the amount of the deposit.

(6) An order made under this rule, and the tribunal's reasons for considering that the

12

contentions in question have no reasonable prospect of success, shall be recorded in summary form in a document signed by the chairman. A copy of that document shall be sent to each of the parties and shall be accompanied by a note explaining that if the party against whom the order is made persists in participating in proceedings relating to the matter to which the order relates, he may have an award of costs made against him and could lose his deposit.

(7) If a party against whom an order has been made does not remit the amount specified in the order to the Secretary either–

(a) within the period of 21 days beginning with the day on which the document recording the making of the order is sent to him, or

(b) within such further period, not exceeding 14 days, as the tribunal may allow in the light of representations made by that party within the said period of 21 days,

the tribunal shall strike out the originating application or notice of appearance of that party or, as the case may be, the part of it to which the order relates.

(8) The deposit paid by a party under an order made under this rule shall be refunded to him in full except where–

(a) the tribunal has found against that party in a decision on the matter in respect of which the party was ordered to pay the deposit; and

(b) an award of costs has been made against that party (whether arising out of the proceedings relating to that matter or out of proceedings relating to any other matter considered with that matter).

(9) No member of a tribunal which has conducted a pre-hearing review shall be a member of the tribunal at the hearing of the originating application.

The hearing

8.—(1) Any hearing of an originating application shall be heard by a tribunal composed in accordance with section 128(2A), (2B) and (2C), or section 128(6), of the 1978 Act.

(2) Any hearing of or in connection with an originating application shall take place in public except where a Minister of the Crown has directed a tribunal to sit in private on grounds of national security in accordance with paragraph 1(4A) of Schedule 9 to the 1978 Act.

(3) Notwithstanding paragraph (2), a tribunal may sit in private for the purpose of–

(a) hearing evidence which in the opinion of the tribunal relates to matters of such a nature that it would be against the interests of national security to allow the evidence to be given in public; or

(b) hearing evidence from any person which in the opinion of the tribunal is likely to consist of–

(i) information which he could not disclose without contravening a prohibition imposed by or under any enactment, or

(ii) any information which has been communicated to him in confidence, or which he has otherwise obtained in consequence of the confidence reposed in him by another person, or

(iii) information the disclosure of which would cause substantial injury to any undertaking of his or any undertaking in which he works for reasons other than its effect on negotiations with respect to any of the matters mentioned in section 244(1) of the 1992 Act.

(4) A member of the Council on Tribunals shall be entitled to attend any hearing taking place in private in his capacity as a member.

(5) If a party wishes to submit representations in writing for consideration by a tribunal at the hearing of the originating application he shall present his representations to the Secretary not less than 7 days before the hearing and shall at the same time send a copy to each other party.

(6) The Secretary of State if he so elects shall be entitled to appear as if he were a party and be heard at any hearing of or in connection with an originating application in proceedings which may involve a payment out of the National Insurance Fund, and in that event he shall be treated for the purposes of these rules as if he were a party.

Procedure at hearing

9.—(1) The tribunal shall, so far as it appears to it appropriate, seek to avoid formality in its proceedings and shall not be bound by any enactment or rule of law relating to the admissibility of evidence in proceedings before the courts of law. The tribunal shall make such enquiries of persons appearing before it and witnesses as it considers appropriate and shall otherwise conduct the

13

hearing in such manner as it considers most appropriate for the clarification of the issues before it and generally to the just handling of the proceedings.

(2) Subject to paragraph (1), at the hearing of the originating application a party shall be entitled to give evidence, to call witnesses, to question any witnesses and to address the tribunal.

(3) If a party fails to attend or to be represented at the time and place fixed for the hearing, the tribunal may, if that party is an applicant, dismiss or, in any case, dispose of the application in the absence of that party or may adjourn the hearing to a later date: provided that before dismissing or disposing of any application in the absence of a party the tribunal shall consider his originating application or notice of appearance, any representations in writing presented by him in pursuance of rule 8(5) and any written answer furnished to the tribunal pursuant to rule 4(3).

(4) A tribunal may require any witness to give evidence on oath or affirmation and for that purpose there may be administered an oath or affirmation in due form.

Decision of tribunal

10.—(1) Where a tribunal is composed of three members its decision may be taken by a majority; and if a tribunal is composed of two members only, the chairman shall have a second or casting vote.

(2) The decision of a tribunal, which may be given orally at the end of a hearing or reserved, shall be recorded in a document signed by the chairman.

(3) The tribunal shall give reasons for its decision in a document signed by the chairman. That document shall contain a statement as to whether the reasons are given in summary or extended form and where the tribunal–

    (a) makes an award of compensation, or

    (b) comes to any other determination by virtue of which one party is required to pay a sum to another (excluding an award of costs or allowances),

the document shall also contain a statement of the amount of compensation awarded, or of the sum required to be paid, followed either by a table showing how the amount or sum has been calculated or by a description of the manner in which it has been calculated.

(4) The reasons for the decision of the tribunal shall be given in summary form except where–

    (a) the proceedings involved the determination of an issue arising under or relating to the 1970 Act, the 1975 Act, the 1986 Act or the 1976 Act;

    (b) a request that the reasons be given in extended form is made orally at the hearing by a party;

    (c) such a request is made in writing by a party after the hearing either–

        (i) before any document recording the reasons in summary form is sent to the parties, or

        (ii) within 21 days of the date on which that document was sent to the parties; or

    (d) the tribunal considers that reasons given in summary form would not sufficiently explain the grounds for its decision;

and in those circumstances the reasons shall be given in extended form.

(5) The clerk shall transmit the documents referred to in paragraphs (2) and (3) to the Secretary who shall enter them in the Register and shall send a copy of the entry to each of the parties and where the proceedings were referred to the tribunal by a court, to that court.

(6) The document referred to in paragraph (3) shall be omitted from the Register in any case in which–

    (a) a Minister of the Crown has directed the tribunal, in accordance with paragraph 1(4A) of Schedule 9 to the 1978 Act, to sit in private on grounds of national security, or

    (b) evidence has been heard in private and the tribunal so directs.

In such a case the Secretary shall send that document to each of the parties; and where there are proceedings before a superior court relating to the decision in question, he shall send the document to that court, together with a copy of the entry in the Register of the document referred to in paragraph (2).

(7) In any case appearing to involve allegations of a sexual offence, the document referred to in paragraph (3) shall be entered on the Register with such deletions or amendments as have been made in accordance with rule 13(6).

(8) The Register shall be kept at the Office of the Tribunals and shall be open to the inspection of any person without charge at all reasonable hours.

14

SCHEDULE 1—*continued*

(9) Clerical mistakes in the documents referred to in paragraphs (2) and (3), or errors arising in those documents from an accidental slip or omission, may at any time be corrected by the chairman by certificate under his hand.

(10) If a document is corrected by certificate under paragraph (9), or if a decision is—

(a) reviewed, revoked or varied by certificate under rule 11, or

(b) altered in any way by order of a superior court,

the Secretary shall alter any entry in the Register which is affected to conform with the certificate or order and send a copy of any entry so altered to each of the parties and, where the proceedings were referred to the tribunal by a court, to that court.

(11) Where a document omitted from the Register pursuant to paragraph (6) is corrected by certificate under paragraph (9), the Secretary shall send a copy of the corrected document to each of the parties; and where there are proceedings before any superior court relating to the decision in question, he shall send a copy to that court together with a copy of the entry in the Register of the document referred to in paragraph (2), if it has been altered under paragraph (10).

(12) Where this rule requires a document to be signed by the chairman of a tribunal composed of three or two persons, but by reason of death or incapacity the chairman is unable to sign it, the document shall be signed by the other members or member of the tribunal, who shall certify that the chairman is unable to sign.

Review of tribunal's decision

11.—(1) Subject to the provisions of this rule, a tribunal shall have power, on the application of a party or of its own motion, to review any decision on the grounds that—

(a) the decision was wrongly made as a result of an error on the part of the tribunal staff;

(b) a party did not receive notice of the proceedings leading to the decision;

(c) the decision was made in the absence of a party;

(d) new evidence has become available since the conclusion of the hearing to which the decision relates, provided that its existence could not have been reasonably known of or foreseen at the time of the hearing; or

(e) the interests of justice require such a review.

(2) A tribunal may not review a decision of its own motion unless it is the tribunal which issued the decision.

(3) A tribunal may only review a decision of its own motion if, within the period beginning with the date of the hearing and ending with the fourteenth day after the date on which the decision was sent to the parties, it has sent notice to each of the parties explaining in summary form the ground upon which and reasons why it is proposed to review the decision and giving them an opportunity to show cause why there should be no review.

(4) An application for the purposes of paragraph (1) may be made at the hearing. If no application is made at the hearing, an application may be made to the Secretary at any time from the date of the hearing until 14 days after the date on which the decision was sent to the parties and must be in writing stating the grounds in full.

(5) An application for the purposes of paragraph (1) may be refused by the President or by the chairman of the tribunal which decided the case or by a Regional Chairman if in his opinion it has no reasonable prospect of success.

(6) If such an application is not refused under paragraph (5) it shall be heard by the tribunal which decided the case, or—

(a) where it is not practicable for it to be heard by that tribunal, or

(b) where the decision was made by a chairman acting alone under rule 13(8),

by a tribunal appointed by either the President or a Regional Chairman.

(7) On reviewing its decision a tribunal may confirm the decision, or vary or revoke the decision under the chairman's hand; and if it revokes the decision, the tribunal shall order a re-hearing before either the same or a differently constituted tribunal.

Costs

12.—(1) Where, in the opinion of the tribunal, a party has in bringing or conducting the proceedings acted frivolously, vexatiously, abusively, disruptively or otherwise unreasonably, the tribunal may make—

(a) an order containing an award against that party in respect of the costs incurred by another party;

15

    (b) an order that that party shall pay to the Secretary of State the whole, or any part, of any allowances (other than allowances paid to members of tribunals) paid by the Secretary of State under paragraph 10 of Schedule 9 to the 1978 Act to any person for the purposes of, or in connection with, his attendance at the tribunal.

(2) Paragraph (1) applies to a respondent who has not entered an appearance in relation to the conduct of any part in the proceedings which he has taken.

(3) An order containing an award against a party ("the first party") in respect of the costs incurred by another party ("the second party") shall be–

    (a) where the tribunal thinks fit, an order that the first party pay to the second party a specified sum not exceeding £500;

    (b) where those parties agree on a sum to be paid by the first party to the second party in respect of those costs, an order that the first party pay to the second party a specified sum, being the sum so agreed; or

    (c) in any other case, an order that the first party pay to the second party the whole or a specified part of the costs incurred by the second party as taxed (if not otherwise agreed).

(4) Where the tribunal has on the application of a party postponed the day or time fixed for or adjourned the hearing, the tribunal may make orders, of the kinds mentioned in paragraphs (1)(a) and (1)(b), against or, as the case may require, in favour of that party as respects any costs incurred or any allowances paid as a result of the postponement or adjournment.

(5) A tribunal shall make orders against a respondent of the kinds mentioned in paragraphs 1(a) and 1(b) as respects any costs or any allowances paid as a result of the postponement or adjournment of a hearing where, on a complaint of unfair dismissal–

    (a) the applicant has expressed a wish to be reinstated or re-engaged which has been communicated to the respondent at least 7 days before the hearing of the complaint, or

    (b) the proceedings arise out of the respondent's failure to permit the applicant to return to work after an absence due to pregnancy or confinement,

and the postponement or adjournment has been caused by the respondent's failure, without a special reason, to adduce reasonable evidence as to the availability of the job from which the applicant was dismissed, or, as the case may be, which she held before her absence, or of comparable or suitable employment.

(6) Any costs required by an order under this rule to be taxed may be taxed in the county court according to such of the scales prescribed by the county court rules for proceedings in the county court as shall be directed by the order.

(7) Where–

    (a) a party has been ordered under rule 7 to pay a deposit as a condition of being permitted to continue to participate in proceedings relating to a matter,

    (b) in respect of that matter, the tribunal has found against that party in its decision, and

    (c) there has been no award of costs made against that party arising out of the proceedings on the matter,

the tribunal shall consider whether to award costs against that party on the ground that he conducted the proceedings relating to the matter unreasonably in persisting in having the matter determined by a tribunal; but the tribunal shall not make an award of costs on that ground unless it has considered the document recording the order under rule 7 and is of the opinion that the reasons which caused the tribunal to find against the party in its decision were substantially the same as the reasons recorded in that document for considering that the contentions of the party had no reasonable prospect of success.

(8) Where an award of costs is made against a party who has had an order under rule 7 made against him (whether the award arises out of the proceedings relating to the matter in respect of which the order was made or out of proceedings relating to any other matter considered with that matter), his deposit shall be paid in part or full settlement of the award–

    (a) where an award is made in favour of one party, to that party, and

    (b) where awards are made in favour of more than one party, to all of them or any one or more of them as the tribunal thinks fit, and if to all or more than one, in such proportions as the tribunal considers appropriate,

and if the amount of the deposit exceeds the amount of the award of costs, the balance shall be refunded to the party who paid it.

Miscellaneous powers

    13.—(1) Subject to the provisions of these rules, a tribunal may regulate its own procedure.

SCHEDULE 1—*continued*

(2) A tribunal may–

    (a) if the applicant at any time gives notice of the withdrawal of his originating application, dismiss the proceedings;

    (b) if both or all the parties agree in writing upon the terms of a decision to be made by the tribunal, decide accordingly;

    (c) consider representations in writing which have been submitted by a party to the Secretary (pursuant to rule 8(5)) less than 7 days before the hearing;

    (d) subject to paragraph (3), at any stage of the proceedings, order to be struck out or amended any originating application or notice of appearance, or anything in such application or notice of appearance, on the grounds that it is scandalous, frivolous or vexatious;

    (e) subject to paragraph (3), at any stage of the proceedings, order to be struck out any originating application or notice of appearance on the grounds that the manner in which the proceedings have been conducted by or on behalf of the applicant or, as the case may be, respondent has been scandalous, frivolous or vexatious; and

    (f) subject to paragraph (3), on the application of the respondent, or of its own motion, order an originating application to be struck out for want of prosecution.

(3) Before making an order under sub-paragraph (d), (e) or (f) of paragraph (2) the tribunal shall send notice to the party against whom it is proposed that the order should be made giving him an opportunity to show cause why the order should not be made; but this paragraph shall not be taken to require the tribunal to send such notice to that party if the party has been given an opportunity to show cause orally why the order should not be made.

(4) Where a notice required by paragraph (3) is sent in relation to an order to strike out an originating application for want of prosecution, service of the notice shall be treated as having been effected if it has been sent by post or delivered in accordance with rule 20(3) and the tribunal may strike out the originating application (notwithstnding that there has been no direction for substituted service in accordance with rule 20(6)) if the party does not avail himself of the opportunity given by the notice.

(5) A tribunal may, before determining an application under rule 4 or rule 17, require the party making the application to give notice of it to every other party. The notice shall give particulars of the application and indicate the address to which and the time within which any objection to the application shall be made, being an address and time specified for the purposes of the application by the tribunal.

(6) In any case appearing to involve allegations of the commission of a sexual offence, the tribunal or the Secretary shall omit from the Register, or delete from the Register or any decision, document or record of the proceedings, which is available to the public, any identifying matter which is likely to lead members of the public to identify any person affected by or making such an allegation.

(7) A chairman may postpone the day or time fixed for, or adjourn, any hearing (particularly where an enactment provides for conciliation in relation to the case, for the purpose of giving an opportunity for the case to be settled by way of conciliation and withdrawn) and vary any such postponement or adjournment.

(8) Any act required or authorised by these rules to be done by a tribunal may be done by a chairman except–

    (a) the hearing of an originating application under rule 8;

    (b) an act required or authorised to be so done by rule 9 or 10 which the rule implies is to be done by the tribunal which is hearing or heard the originating application;

    (c) the review of a decision under rule 11(1), and the confirmation, variation or revocation of a decision, and ordering of a re-hearing, under rule 11(6).

(9) Any act required or authorised by rules 3(4) and (5), 13(7) and 15 to be done by a chairman may be done by a tribunal or on the direction of a chairman.

(10) Any function of the Secretary may be performed by a Regional Secretary or by a person acting with the authority of the Secretary or of a Regional Secretary.

Restricted reporting orders

14.—(1) In any case which involves allegations of sexual misconduct the tribunal may at any time before promulgation of its decision in respect of an originating application, either on the application of a party made by notice to the Secretary or of its own motion, make a restricted reporting order.

17

SCHEDULE 1—*continued*

(2) The tribunal shall not make a restricted reporting order unless it has given each party an opportunity to advance oral argument at a hearing, if they so wish.

(3) Where a tribunal makes a restricted reporting order–

    (a) it shall specify in the order the persons who may not be identified;

    (b) the order shall remain in force until the promulgation of the decision of the tribunal on the originating application to which it relates unless revoked earlier; and

    (c) the Regional Secretary shall ensure that a notice of that fact is displayed on the notice board of the tribunal with any list of the proceedings taking place before the industrial tribunal, and on the door of the room in which the proceedings affected by the order are taking place.

(4) A tribunal may revoke a restricted reporting order at any time if it thinks fit.

(5) For the purposes of this rule "promulgation" occurs on the date recorded as being the date on which the document recording the determination of the originating application was sent to the parties.

Extension of time

15.—(1) A chairman may on the application of a party or of his own motion extend the time for doing any act appointed by or under these rules (including this rule) and may do so whether or not the time so appointed has expired.

(2) An application under paragraph (1) shall be made by presenting to the Secretary a notice of application, which shall state the title of the proceedings and shall set out the grounds of the application.

(3) The Secretary shall give notice to each of the parties of any extension of time granted under this rule.

Directions

16.—(1) A tribunal may at any time, on the application of a party or of its own motion, give directions on any matter arising in connection with the proceedings.

(2) An application under paragraph (1) shall be made by presenting to the Secretary a notice of application, which shall state the title of the proceedings and set out the grounds of the application.

Joinder and representative respondents

17.—(1) A tribunal may at any time, on the application of any person made by notice to the Secretary or of its own motion, direct any person against whom any relief is sought to be joined as a party, and give such consequential directions as it considers necessary.

(2) A tribunal may likewise, on such application or of its own motion, order that any respondent named in the originating application or subsequently added, who appears to the tribunal not to have been, or to have ceased to be, directly interested in the subject of the originating application, be dismissed from the proceedings.

(3) Where a number of persons having the same interest in an originating application, one or more of them may be cited as the person or persons against whom relief is sought, or may be authorised by the tribunal, before or at the hearing, to defend on behalf of all the persons so interested.

Combined proceedings

18.—(1) Where, in relation to two or more originating applications pending before the industrial tribunals, it appears to an industrial tribunal, on the application of a party made by notice to the Secretary or of its own motion, that–

    (a) a common question of law or fact arises in some or all the originating applications, or

    (b) the relief claimed in some or all of those originating applications is in respect of or arises out of the same set of facts, or

    (c) for any other reason it is desirable to make an order under this rule,

the tribunal may order that some (as specified in the order) or all of the originating applications in respect of which it so appears to the tribunal shall be considered together, and may give such consequential directions as may be necessary.

(2) The tribunal shall only make an order under this rule if–

    (a) each of the parties concerned has been given an opportunity at a hearing to show cause why such an order should not be made; or

18

SCHEDULE 1—*continued*

(b) it has sent notice to all the parties concerned giving them an opportunity to show such cause.

(3) The tribunal may, on the application of a party made by notice to the Secretary or of its own motion, vary or set aside an order made under this rule but shall not do so unless it has given each party an opportunity to make either oral or written representations before the order is varied or set aside.

Transfer of proceedings

19.—(1) On the application of a party made by notice to the Secretary or of his own motion, the President or a Regional Chairman may at any time, with the consent of the President of the Industrial Tribunals (Scotland), direct any proceedings to be transferred to the Office of the Industrial Tribunals (Scotland) if it appears to him that the proceedings could be, and would more conveniently be, determined in an industrial tribunal (Scotland) established in pursuance of the Industrial Tribunals (Constitution and Procedure) (Scotland) Regulations 1993(**a**); but no such direction shall be made unless notice has been sent to all parties concerned giving them an opportunity to show cause why a direction should not be made.

(2) Where proceedings have been transferred to the Office of the Industrial Tribunals (England and Wales) under rule 19(1) of the Industrial Tribunals Rules of Procedure (Scotland) 1993 they shall be treated as if in all respects they had been commenced by an originating application pursuant to rule 1.

Notices, etc.

20.—(1) Any notice given under these rules shall be in writing.

(2) All notices and documents required by these rules to be presented to the Secretary may be presented at the Office of the Tribunals or such other office as may be notified by the Secretary to the parties.

(3) All notices and documents required or authorised by these rules to be sent or given to any person hereinafter mentioned may be sent by post (subject to paragraph (5)) or delivered to or at–

(a) in the case of a notice or document directed to the Secretary of State in proceedings to which he is not a party (or in respect of which he is treated as a party for the purposes of these rules by virtue of rule 8(6)), the offices of the Department of Employment (Redundancy and Insolvency Branch) at Caxton House, Tothill Street, London SW1H 9NF, or such other office as may be notified by the Secretary of State;

(b) in the case of a notice or document directed to a court, the office of the clerk of the court;

(c) in the case of a notice or document directed to a party–

(i) the address specified in his originating application or notice of appearance to which notices and documents are to be sent, or in a notice under paragraph (4), or

(ii) if no such address has been specified, or if a notice sent to such an address has been returned, to any other known address or place of business in the United Kingdom or, if the party is a corporate body, the body's registered or principal office in the United Kingdom, or, in any case, such address or place outside the United Kingdom as the President or a Regional Chairman may allow;

(d) in the case of a notice or document directed to any person (other than a person specified in the foregoing provisions of this paragraph), his address or place of business in the United Kingdom or, if the person is a corporate body, the body's registered or principal office in the United Kingdom;

and a notice or document sent or given to the authorised representative of a party shall be deemed to have been sent or given to that party.

(4) A party may at any time by notice to the Secretary and to the other party or parties (and, where appropriate, to the appropriate concilation officer) change the address to which notices and documents are to be sent.

(5) The recorded delivery service shall be used instead of the ordinary post–

(a) when a second set of notices or documents is sent to a respondent who has not entered an appearance under rule 3(1); and

(b) for service of an order made under rule 4(2).

(6) The President or a Regional Chairman may direct that there shall be substituted service in such manner as he may deem fit in any case he considers appropriate.

(**a**) S.I. 1993/2688.

19

SCHEDULE 1—*continued*

(7) In proceedings brought under the provisions of any enactment providing for concilation the Secretary shall send copies of all documents and notices to a conciliation officer who in the opinion of the Secretary is an appropriate officer to receive them.

(8) In proceedings which may involve a payment out of the National Insurance Fund, the Secretary shall, where appropriate, send copies of all documents and notices to the Secretary of State whether or not he is a party.

(9) In proceedings under the 1970 Act, the 1975 Act or the 1986 Act, or the 1976 Act, the Secretary shall send to the Equal Opportunities Commission or, as the case may be, the Commission for Racial Equality copies of every document and copy entry sent to the parties under rules 10(5) and 10(10).

20

SCHEDULE 2 [Regulation 8(2)]

COMPLEMENTARY RULES OF PROCEDURE

For use only in proceedings involving an equal value claim

Power to require further particulars and attendance of witnesses and to grant discovery

4.—(1) A tribunal may, on the application of a party made either by notice to the Secretary or at the hearing of the originating application, or of its own motion–

    (a) require a party to furnish in writing to the person specified by the tribunal further particulars of the grounds on which that party relies and of any facts and contentions relevant thereto,

    (b) require one party to grant to another such discovery or inspection (including the taking of copies) of documents as might be granted by a county court,

and may appoint the time at or within which and the place at which any act required in pursuance of this rule is to be done.

(2) A tribunal may, on the application of a party made either by notice to the Secretary or at the hearing of the originating application, or of its own motion–

    (a) require the attendance of any person, including a party, as a witness, wherever such person may be within Great Britain, and

    (b) if it does so require the attendance of a person, require him to produce any document relating to the matter to be determined,

and may appoint the time and place at which the person is to attend and, where appropriate, the time at or within which and the place at which any such document is to be produced.

(2A) Subject to paragraph (2B), a tribunal may, on the application of an expert who has been required by the tribunal to prepare a report–

    (a) require any person who the tribunal is satisfied may have information which may be relevant to the question or matter on which the expert is required to report to furnish, in writing, such information as the tribunal may require;

    (b) require any person to produce any documents which are in the possession, custody or power of that person and which the tribunal is satisfied may contain matter relevant to the question on which the expert is required to report;

and any information so required to be furnished or document so required to be produced shall be furnished or produced, at or within such time as the tribunal may appoint, to the Secretary who shall send the information or document to the expert.

(2B) A tribunal shall not make a requirement under paragraph (2A)–

    (a) of a concilation officer who has acted in connection with the complaint under section 64 of the 1975 Act, or

    (b) if it is satisfied that the person so required would have good grounds for refusing to comply with the requirement if it were a requirement made in connection with a hearing before the tribunal.

(3) A tribunal may, on the application of a party made by notice to the Secretary or of its own motion, require a party in writing to furnish to the tribunal a written answer to any question if it considers–

    (a) that the answer of the party to that question may help to clarify any issue likely to arise for determination in the proceedings, and

    (b) that it would be likely to assist the progress of the proceedings for that answer to be available to the tribunal before the hearing,

and may appoint the time within which the written answer is to be furnished. Upon the imposition of such a requirement, the Secretary shall send a copy of the requirement to each other party; and he shall send a copy of the answer to each other party.

(4) The tribunal shall take account of a written answer furnished pursuant to paragraph (3) in the same way as it takes account of representations in writing presented by a party pursuant to rule 8(5).

(5) Where a requirement has been imposed under paragraph (1), (2) or (3)–

    (a) on a party in his absence; or

    (b) on a person other than a party,

that party or person may make an application to the tribunal to vary or set aside the requirement by notice to the Secretary given before the time at which or, as the case may be, the expiration of the time within which the requirement is to be complied with; and the Secretary shall give notice of

21

the application to each party or, where applicable, to each party other than the party making the application.

(5A) A person, whether or not a party, upon whom a requirement has been made under paragraph (2A), may apply to the tribunal by notice to the Secretary before the appointed time at or within which the requirement is to be complied with to vary or set aside the requirement. Notice of such application shall be given to the parties and to the expert upon whose application the requirement was made.

(6) Every document containing a requirement imposed under paragraph (1)(b), (2) or (2A) shall contain a reference to the fact that, under paragraph 1(7) of Schedule 9 to the 1978 Act, any person who without reasonable excuse fails to comply with any such requirement shall be liable on summary conviction to a fine, and the document shall state the amount of the current maximum fine.

(7) If a requirement under paragraph (1) or (3) is not complied with, a tribunal, before or at the hearing, may strike out the whole or part of the originating application, or, as the case may be, of the notice of appearance, and, where appropriate, direct that a respondent shall be debarred from defending altogether: but a tribunal shall not so strike out or direct unless it has sent notice to the party who has not complied with the requirement giving him an opportunity to show cause why the tribunal should not do so.

Procedure relating to expert's report

8A.—(1) In any case involving an equal value claim where a dispute arises as to whether any work is of equal value to other work in terms of the demands made on the person employed on the work (for instance under such headings as effort, skill and decision) (in this rule hereinafter referred to as "the question"), a tribunal shall, before considering the question, except in cases to which section 2A(1)(a) of the Equal Pay Act applies, require an expert to prepare a report with respect to the question and the requirement shall be made in accordance with paragraphs (2) and (3).

(2) The requirement shall be made in writing and shall set out–
  (a) the name and address of each of the parties;
  (b) the address of the establishment at which the applicant is (or, as the case may be, was) employed;
  (c) the question; and
  (d) the identity of the person with reference to whose work the question arises;
and a copy of the requirement shall be sent to each of the parties.

(3) The requirement shall stipulate that the expert shall–
  (a) take account of all such information supplied and all such representations made to him as have a bearing on the question;
  (b) before drawing up his report, produce and send to the parties a written summary of the said information and representations and invite the representations of the parties upon the material contained therein;
  (c) make his report to the tribunal in a document which shall reproduce the summary and contain a brief account of any representations received from the parties upon it, any conclusion he may have reached upon the question and the reasons for that conclusion or, as the case may be, for his failure to reach such a conclusion;
  (d) take no account of the difference of sex and at all times act fairly.

(4) Where a tribunal requires an expert to prepare a report, it shall adjourn the hearing.

(5) The expert shall, either within 14 days of receiving the requirement or, where paragraph (6) applies, as soon as practicable thereafter, give notice in writing to the Secretary of the date by which he expects to send his report to the tribunal, and the Secretary shall send a copy of the notice to each party.

(6) If the expert considers that he is unable to determine the date referred to in paragraph (5) within the period of 14 days mentioned in that paragraph, he shall promptly give notice in writing to the Secretary of the reasons for his inability to determine that date and of the date by which he expects to be able to send the notice mentioned in that paragraph. The Secretary shall send a copy of any notice sent under this paragraph to each party.

(7) In paragraphs (8), (9) and (10), "the projected date" means the date most recently specified by the expert, in a notice given under paragraph (5) or (8) or in a progress report sent to the tribunal under paragraph (9), as the date by which he expects to send his report to the tribunal.

22

SCHEDULE 2—*continued*

(8) If at any time the expert considers that there will be a material delay in sending his report to the tribunal beyond the projected date, he shall give notice in writing to the Secretary of–

   (a) that fact,
   (b) the date by which he now expects to send his report to the tribunal, and
   (c) the reasons for the delay including, in particular, whether he considers that any actions or failures to act by a party have, in whole or in part, caused the delay.

The Secretary shall send a copy of any such notice to each party.

(9) At any time before the tribunal receives the report of the expert the tribunal may, acting on the request of a party or otherwise, require the expert to send a progress report to the tribunal. If so required, the expert shall, as soon as practicable–

   (a) if he receives the requirement before the projected date and has not sent his report, prepare and send to the tribunal a progress report–
      (i) stating whether he considers that there will be any material delay in sending his report to the tribunal beyond the projected date, and
      (ii) if he considers that there will be such a delay, giving the reasons for the delay and stating the date by which he now expects to send his report to the tribunal;
   (b) if he receives the requirement on or after the projected date and has not sent his report, prepare and send to the tribunal a progress report giving the reasons for the delay in sending his report and stating the date by which he now expects to send his report to the tribunal;
   (c) if he has sent his report to the tribunal, notify the Secretary of that fact.

The Secretary shall send a copy of any progress report sent to the tribunal under this rule to each party.

(10) If a tribunal considers that–

   (a) the projected date specified in a notice given under paragraph (5) indicates that the expert will take longer than is appropriate to prepare his report, or
   (b) the projected date specified in a notice given under paragraph (8) or in a progress report sent to the tribunal under paragraph (9) indicates that there will be an unjustifiable delay beyond the previous projected date,

the tribunal may, after seeking representations from the parties and if it considers that it would be in the interests of justice to replace the expert, revoke, by notice in writing to the expert, the requirement to prepare a report; and in that event paragraph (1) shall again apply.

(11) Where a tribunal has received the report of an expert, it shall send a copy of the report to each party and fix a date for the hearing of the case to be resumed; and the date so fixed shall be the earliest reasonably practicable date after the expiration of 14 days from the date on which the report is sent to the parties.

(12) Upon the resumption of the hearing of the case in accordance with paragraph (11) the report shall be admitted as evidence in the case unless the tribunal has exercised its power under paragraph (13) not to admit the report.

(13) Where the tribunal, on the application of one or more of the parties or otherwise, forms the view–

   (a) that the expert has not complied with a stipulation in paragraph (3), or
   (b) that the conclusion contained in the report is one which, taking due account of the information supplied and representations made to the expert, could not reasonably have been reached, or
   (c) that for some other material reason (other than disagreement with the conclusion that the applicant's work is or is not of equal value or with the reasoning leading to that conclusion) the report is unsatisfactory,

the tribunal, may if it thinks fit, determine not to admit the report, and in such a case paragraph (1) shall again apply.

(14) In forming its view on the matters contained in paragraph (13)(a), (b) and (c) the tribunal shall take account of any representations of the parties thereon and may in that connection, subject to rule 9(2A) and (2B), permit any party to give evidence upon, to call witnesses and to question any witness upon any matter relevant thereto.

(15) The tribunal may, at any time after it has received the report of an expert, require that expert (or, if that is impracticable, another expert) to explain any matter contained in that report or, having regard to such matters as may be set out in the requirement, to give further consideration to the question.

23

SCHEDULE 2—*continued*

(16) A requirement under paragraph (15) shall be made in accordance with paragraph (2) and shall stipulate that the expert shall make his reply in writing to the tribunal, giving his explanation or, as the case may be, setting down any conclusion which may result from his further consideration and his reasons for that conclusion.

(17) Where the tribunal has received a reply from the expert under paragraph (16), it shall send a copy of the reply to each of the parties and shall allow the parties to make representations thereon, and the reply shall be treated as information furnished to the tribunal and be given such weight as the tribunal thinks fit.

(18) Where a tribunal has determined not to admit a report under paragraph (13), that report shall be treated for all purposes (other than the award of costs or allowances under rule 12) connected with the proceedings as if it had not been received by the tribunal and no further account shall be taken of it, and the requirement on the expert to prepare a report shall lapse.

Procedure at hearing

9.—(1) The tribunal shall, so far as it appears to it appropriate, seek to avoid formality in its proceedings and shall not be bound by any enactment or rule of law relating to the admissibility of evidence in proceedings before the courts of law. The tribunal shall make such enquiries of persons appearing before it and witnesses as it considers appropriate and, subject to paragraphs (2A), (2B), (2C), (2D) and (2E), shall otherwise conduct the hearing in such manner as it considers most suitable to the clarification of the issues before it and generally to the just handling of the proceedings.

(2) Subject to paragraphs (1), (2A), (2B), (2C) and (2D), at the hearing of the originating application a party shall be entitled to give evidence, to call witnesses, to question any witnesses and to address the tribunal.

(2A) The tribunal may, and shall upon the application of a party, require the attendance of an expert who has prepared a report in connection with an equal value claim in any hearing relating to that claim. Where an expert attends in compliance with such requirement any party may, subject to paragraph (1), cross-examine the expert on his report and on any other matter pertaining to the question on which the expert was required to report.

(2B) At any time after the tribunal has received the report of the expert, any party may, on giving reasonable notice of his intention to do so to the tribunal and to any other party to the claim, call one witness to give expert evidence on the question on which the tribunal has required the expert to prepare a report; and where such evidence is given, any other party may cross-examine the person giving that evidence upon it.

(2C) Except as provided in rule 8A(14) or by paragraph (2D), no party may give evidence upon, or question any witness upon, any matter of fact upon which a conclusion in the report of the expert is based.

(2D) Subject to paragraphs (2A) and (2B), a tribunal may, notwithstanding paragraph (2C), permit a party to give evidence upon, to call witnesses and to question any witness upon any such matters of fact as are referred to in paragraph (2C) if either–

(a) the matter of fact is relevant to and is raised in connection with the issue contained in subsection (3) of section 1 of the Equal Pay Act (defence of genuine material factor) upon which the determination of the tribunal is being sought; or

(b) the report of the expert contains no conclusion on the question of whether the applicant's work and the work of the person identified in the requirement of the tribunal under rule 8A(2) are of equal value and the tribunal is satisfied that the absence of that conclusion is wholly or mainly due to the refusal or deliberate omission of a person required by the tribunal under rule 4(1A) to furnish information or to produce documents to comply with that requirement.

(2E) A tribunal may, on the application of a party, if in the circumstances of the case, having regard to the considerations expressed in paragraph (1), it considers that it is appropriate so to proceed, hear evidence upon and permit the parties to address it upon the issue contained in subsection (3) of section 1 of the Equal Pay Act (defence of genuine material factor) before it requires an expert to prepare a report under rule 8A. Where the tribunal so proceeds, it shall be without prejudice to further consideration of that issue after the tribunal has received the report.

(3) If a party fails to attend or to be represented at the time and place fixed for the hearing, the tribunal may, if that party is an applicant, dismiss or, in any case, dispose of the application in the absence of that party or may adjourn the hearing to a later date: provided that before dismissing or disposing of any application in the absence of a party the tribunal shall consider his originating application or notice of appearance, any representations in writing presented by him in pursuance of rule 8(5) and any written answer furnished to the tribunal pursuant to rule 4(3).

24

(4) A tribunal may require any witness to give evidence on oath or affirmation and for that purpose there may be administered an oath or affirmation in due form.

Decision of tribunal

10.—(1) Where a tribunal is composed of three members its decision may be taken by a majority; and if a tribunal is composed of two members only, the chairman shall have a second or casting vote.

(2) The decision of a tribunal, which may be given orally at the end of a hearing or reserved, shall be recorded in a document signed by the chairman.

(3) The tribunal shall give reasons for its decision in extended form in a document signed by the chairman; and where the tribunal–

(a) makes an award of compensation, or

(b) comes to any other determination by virtue of which one party is required to pay a sum to another (excluding an award of costs or allowances),

the document shall also contain a statement of the amount of compensation awarded, or of the sum required to be paid, followed either by a table showing how the amount or sum has been calculated or by a description of the manner in which it has been calculated.

[paragraph (4) is omitted because it has no relevance in proceedings involving an equal value claim]

(4A) There shall be appended to the document referred to in paragraph (3) a copy of the report (if any) of an expert received by the tribunal in the course of the proceedings.

(5) The clerk shall transmit the documents referred to in paragraphs (2) and (3) and the copy of the report referred to in paragraph (4A), if any, to the Secretary who shall enter them in the Register and shall send a copy of the entry to each of the parties and where the proceedings were referred to the tribunal by a court, to that court.

(6) The document referred to in paragraph (3) and the copy of the report referred to in paragraph (4A), if any, shall be omitted from the Register in any case in which–

(a) a Minister of the Crown has directed the tribunal, in accordance with paragraph 1(4A) of Schedule 9 to the 1978 Act, to sit in private on grounds of national security, or

(b) evidence had been heard in private and the tribunal so directs.

In such a case the Secretary shall send that document to each of the parties; and where there are proceedings before a superior court relating to the decision in question, he shall send the document to that court, together with a copy of the entry in the Register of the document referred to in paragraph (2).

(7) In any case appearing to involve allegations of a sexual offence, the document referred to in paragraph (3) shall be entered on the Register with such deletions or amendments as have been made in accordance with rule 13(6).

(8) The Register shall be kept at the Office of the Tribunals and shall be open to the inspection of any person without charge at all reasonable hours.

(9) Clerical mistakes in the documents referred to in paragraphs (2) and (3), or errors arising in those documents from an accidental slip or omission, may at any time be corrected by the chairman by certificate under his hand.

(10) If a document is corrected by certificate under paragraph (9), or if a decision is–

(a) reviewed, revoked or varied by certificate under rule 11, or

(b) altered in any way by order of a superior court,

the Secretary shall alter any entry in the Register which is affected to conform with the certificate or order and send a copy of any entry so altered to each of the parties and, where the proceedings were referred to the tribunal by a court, to that court.

(11) Where a document omitted from the Register pursuant to paragraph (6) is corrected by certificate under paragraph (9), the Secretary shall send a copy of the corrected document to each of the parties; and where there are proceedings before any superior court relating to the decision in question, he shall send a copy to that court together with a copy of the entry in the Register of the document referred to in paragraph (2), if it has been altered under paragraph (10).

(12) Where this rule requires a document to be signed by the chairman of a tribunal composed of three or two persons, but by reason of death or incapacity the chairman is unable to sign it, the document shall be signed by the other members or member of the tribunal, who shall certify that the chairman is unable to sign.

25

SCHEDULE 2—*continued*

Costs

12.—(1) Where, in the opinion of the tribunal, a party has in bringing or conducting the proceedings acted frivolously, vexatiously, abusively, disruptively or otherwise unreasonably, the tribunal may make–

(a) an order containing an award against that party in respect of the costs incurred by another party;

(b) an order that that party shall pay to the Secretary of State the whole, or any part, of any allowances (other than allowances paid to members of tribunals) paid by the Secretary of State under paragraph 10 of Schedule 9 to the 1978 Act to any person for the purposes of, or in connection with, his attendance at the tribunal.

(2) Paragraph (1) applies to a respondent who has not entered an appearance in relation to the conduct of any part in the proceedings which he has taken.

(2A) For the purposes of paragraph (1)(a), the costs in respect of which a tribunal may make an order include costs incurred by the party in whose favour the order is to be made in or in connection with the investigations carried out by the expert in preparing his report.

(3) An order containing an award against a party ("the first party") in respect of the costs incurred by another party ("the second party") shall be –

(a) where the tribunal thinks fit, an order that the first party pay to the second party a specified sum not exceeding £500;

(b) where those parties agree on a sum to be paid by the first party to the second party in respect of those costs, an order that the first party pay to the second party a specified sum, being the sum so agreed; or

(c) in any other case, an order that the first party pay to the second party the whole or a specified part of the costs incurred by the second party as taxed (if not otherwise agreed).

(4) Where the tribunal has on the application of a party postponed the day or time fixed for or adjourned the hearing, the tribunal may make orders, of the kinds mentioned in paragraphs (1)(a) and (1)(b), against or, as the case may require, in favour of that party as respects any costs incurred or any allowances paid as a result of the postponement or adjournment.

(5) A tribunal shall make orders against a respondent of the kinds mentioned in paragraphs 1(a) and 1(b) as respects any costs or any allowances paid as a result of the postponement or adjournment of a hearing where, on a complaint of unfair dismissal–

(a) the applicant has expressed a wish to be reinstated or re-engaged which has been communicated to the respondent at least 7 days before the hearing of the complaint, or

(b) the proceedings arise out of the respondent's failure to permit the applicant to return to work after an absence due to pregnancy or confinement,

and the postponement or adjournment has been caused by the respondent's failure, without a special reason, to adduce reasonable evidence as to the availability of the job from which the applicant was dismissed, or, as the case may be, which she held before her absence, or of comparable or suitable employment.

(6) Any costs required by an order under this rule to be taxed may be taxed in the county court according to such of the scales prescribed by the county court rules for proceedings in the county court as shall be directed by the order.

(7) Where–

(a) a party has been ordered under rule 7 to pay a deposit as a condition of being permitted to continue to participate in proceedings relating to a matter,

(b) in respect of that matter, the tribunal has found against that party in its decision, and

(c) there has been no award of costs made against that party arising out of the proceedings on the matter,

the tribunal shall consider whether to award costs against that party on the ground that he conducted the proceedings relating to the matter unreasonably in persisting in having the matter determined by a tribunal; but the tribunal shall not make an award of costs on that ground unless it has considered the document recording the order under rule 7 and is of the opinion that the reasons which caused the tribunal to find against the party in its decision were substantially the same as the reasons recorded in that document for considering that the contentions of the party had no reasonable prospect of success.

(8) Where an award of costs is made against a party who has had an order under rule 7 made against him (whether the award arises out of the proceedings relating to the matter in respect of which the order was made or out of proceedings relating to any other matter considered with that matter), his deposit shall be paid in part or full settlement of the award–

26

SCHEDULE 2—*continued*
 (a) where an award is made in favour of one party, to that party, and
 (b) where awards are made in favour of more than one party, to all of them or any one or more of them as the tribunal thinks fit, and if to all or more than one, in such proportions as the tribunal considers appropriate,

and if the amount of the deposit exceeds the amount of the award of costs, the balance shall be refunded to the party who paid it.

Miscellaneous powers

13.—(1) Subject to the provisions of these rules, a tribunal may regulate its own procedure.

(2) A tribunal may–
 (a) if the applicant at any time gives notice of the withdrawal of his originating application, dismiss the proceedings;
 (b) if both or all the parties agree in writing upon the terms of a decision to be made by the tribunal, decide accordingly;
 (c) consider representations in writing which have been submitted by a party to the Secretary (pursuant to rule 8(5)) less than 7 days before the hearing;
 (d) subject to paragraph (3), at any stage of the proceedings, order to be struck out or amended any originating application or notice of appearance, or anything in such application or notice of appearance, on the grounds that it is scandalous, frivolous or vexatious;
 (e) subject to paragraph (3), at any stage of the proceedings, order to be struck out any originating application or notice of appearance on the grounds that the manner in which the proceedings have been conducted by or on behalf of the applicant or, as the case may be, respondent has been scandalous, frivolous or vexatious; and
 (f) subject to paragraph (3), on the application of the respondent, or of its own motion, order an originating application to be struck out for want of prosecution.

(3) Before making an order under sub-paragraph (d), (e) or (f) of paragraph (2) the tribunal shall send notice to the party against whom it is proposed that the order should be made giving him an opportunity to show cause why the order should not be made; but this paragraph shall not be taken to require the tribunal to send such notice to that party if the party has been given an opportunity to show cause orally why the order should not be made.

(4) Where a notice required by paragraph (3) is sent in relation to an order to strike out an originating application for want of prosecution, service of the notice shall be treated as having been effected if it has been sent by post or delivered in accordance with rule 20(3) and the tribunal may strike out the originating application (notwithstanding that there has been no direction for substituted service in accordance with rule 20(6)) if the party does not avail himself of the opportunity given by the notice.

(5) A tribunal may, before determining an application under rule 4 or rule 17, require the party making the application or, in the case of an application under rule 4(2A), the expert, to give notice of it to every other party (or, in the case of an application by the expert, to the parties and any other person on whom the tribunal is asked, in the application, to impose a requirement). The notice shall give particulars of the application and indicate the address to which and the time within which any objection to the application shall be made, being an address and time specified for the purposes of the application by the tribunal.

(6) In any case appearing to involve allegations of the commission of a sexual offence, the tribunal or the Secretary shall omit from the Register, or delete from the Register or any decision, document or record of the proceedings, which is available to the public, any identifying matter which is likely to lead members of the public to identify any person affected by or making such an allegation.

(6A) Without prejudice to paragraph (7), the tribunal shall, before proceeding to hear the parties on an equal value claim, invite them to apply for an adjournment for the purpose of seeking to reach a settlement of the claim and shall, if both or all the parties agree to such a course, grant an adjournment for that purpose.

(6B) If, after the tribunal has adjourned the hearing under rule 8A(4) but before the tribunal has received the report of the expert, the applicant gives notice under paragraph (2)(a), the tribunal shall notify the expert that the requirement to prepare a report has ceased. The notice shall be without prejudice to the operation of rule 12(2A).

(7) A chairman may postpone the day or time fixed for, or adjourn, any hearing (particularly where an enactment provides for conciliation in relation to the case, for the purpose of giving an opportunity for the case to be settled by way of conciliation and withdrawn) and vary any such postponement or adjournment.

27

SCHEDULE 2—*continued*

(8) Any act required or authorised by these rules to be done by a tribunal may be done by a chairman except–

    (a) the hearing of an originating application under rule 8;

    (b) an act required or authorised to be so done by rule 9 or 10 which the rule implies is to be done by the tribunal which is hearing or heard the originating application;

    (c) the review of a decision under rule 11(1), and the confirmation, variation or revocation of a decision, and ordering of a re-hearing, under rule 11(6).

(9) Any act required or authorised by rules 3(4) and (5), 13(7) and 15 to be done by a chairman may be done by a tribunal or on the direction of a chairman.

(10) Any function of the Secretary may be performed by a Regional Secretary or by a person acting with the authority of the Secretary or of a Regional Secretary.

Notices, etc.

20.—(1) Any notice given under these rules shall be in writing.

(2) All notices and documents required by these rules to be presented to the Secretary may be presented at the Office of the Tribunals or such other office as may be notified by the Secretary to the parties.

(3) All notices and documents required or authorised by these rules to be sent or given to any person hereinafter mentioned may be sent by post (subject to paragraph (5)) or delivered to or at–

    (a) in the case of a notice or document directed to the Secretary of State in proceedings to which he is not a party (or in respect of which he is treated as a party for the purposes of these rules by virtue of rule 8(6)), the offices of the Department of Employment (Redundancy and Insolvency Branch) at Caxton House, Tothill Street, London SW1H 9NF, or such other office as may be notified by the Secretary of State;

    (b) in the case of a notice or document directed to a court, the office of the clerk of the court;

    (c) in the case of a notice or document directed to a party–

        (i) the address specified in his originating appliction or notice of appearance to which notices and documents are to be sent, or in a notice under paragraph (4), or

        (ii) if no such address has been specified, or if a notice sent to such an address has been returned, to any other known address or place of business in the United Kingdom or, if the party is a corporate body, the body's registered or principal office in the United Kingdom, or, in any case, such address or place outside the United Kingdom as the President or a Regional Chairman may allow;

    (d) in the case of a notice or document directed to any person (other than a person specified in the foregoing provisions of this paragraph), his address or place of business in the United Kingdom or, if the person is a corporate body, the body's registered or principal office in the United Kingdom;

and a notice or document sent or given to the authorised representative of a party shall be deemed to have been sent or given to that party.

(4) A party may at any time by notice to the Secretary and to the other party or parties (and, where appropriate, to the appropriate conciliation officer) change the address to which notices and documents are to be sent.

(5) The recorded delivery service shall be used instead of the ordinary post–

    (a) when a second set of notices or documents is sent to a respondent who has not entered an appearance under rule 3(1); and

    (b) for service of an order made under rule 4(2) or (2A).

(6) The President or a Regional Chairman may direct that there shall be substituted service in such manner as he may deem fit in any case he considers appropriate.

(7) In proceedings brought under the provisions of any enactment providing for conciliation the Secretary shall send copies of all documents and notices to a conciliation officer who in the opinion of the Secretary is an appropriate officer to receive them.

(8) In proceedings which may involve a payment out of the National Insurance Fund, the Secretary shall, where appropriate, send copies of all documents and notices to the Secretary of State whether or not he is a party.

(9) In proceedings under the 1970 Act, the 1975 Act or the 1986 Act, or the 1976 Act, the Secretary shall send to the Equal Opportunities Commission or, as the case may be, the Commission for Racial Equality copies of every document and copy entry sent to the parties under rules 10(5) and 10(10).

28

RULES OF PROCEDURE

APPLICABLE TO APPEALS UNDER LEVY ORDERS

Notice of appeal

1. An appeal against an assessment to a levy shall be instituted by the appellant sending to the Board in duplicate a notice of appeal which shall be substantially in accordance with Form 1, and shall set out the grounds of the appeal.

Action upon receipt of appeal

2.—(1) Subject to the provisions of rules 3 and 4, the Board upon receiving the notice of appeal shall send within 21 days to the Secretary–

    (a) one copy of the notice of appeal;

    (b) a copy of the assessment notice and of any notice by the Board allowing further time for appealing;

    (c) a notice giving the Board's address for service under these rules where that address is different from the address specified in the assessment notice as the address for service of a notice of appeal; and

    (d) any representations in writing relating to the appeal that the Board may then desire to submit to the tribunal.

(2) Failure to comply with any provision of this rule or rule 3 shall not render the appeal or anything done in pursuance thereof invalid.

Further particulars of appeal

3.—(1) Subject to rule 4, this rule applies in a case where the Board upon receiving the notice of appeal requires further particulars of the grounds on which the appellant intends to rely and of any facts and contentions relevant thereto.

(2) The Board shall within 21 days of receiving the notice of appeal send to the appellant a notice specifying the further particulars required by the Board.

(3) The appellant shall within 21 days of receiving the said notice, or within such further period as the Board may allow, send to the Board in duplicate such further particulars.

(4) Subject to the provisions of paragraph (5), the Board shall, within 21 days of receiving such further particulars, send to the Secretary–

    (a) the documents specified in rule 2;

    (b) a copy of the notice requiring the further particulars; and

    (c) such further particulars, and any representations in writing with respect thereto that the Board may then desire to submit to the tribunal.

(5) If such further particulars are not received by the Board in due time, the documents mentioned in sub-paragraphs (a) and (b) of paragraph (4) shall be sent by the Board to the Secretary not later than–

    (a) the fiftieth day after the receipt of the notice of appeal by the Board; or

    (b) if the Board has allowed a further period of time for delivery of further particulars under paragraph (3), the seventh day after the expiration of that period.

Withdrawal of appeal or assessment

4.—(1) The appellant may withdraw the notice of appeal by notice given to the Board at any time before the entry of the appeal in the Register under rule 5(a) and in that event no further action shall be taken in relation to the appeal.

(2) Where an assessment is withdrawn by the Board, no further action shall be taken in relation to the appeal.

Entry of appeal

5. Upon receiving from the Board the relevant documents in accordance with rule 2(1), 3(4) or 3(5) the Secretary shall as soon as practicable–

    (a) enter particulars of the appeal in the Register;

    (b) give notice to the appellant and to the Board of the case number of the appeal entered in the Register (which shall thereafter constitute the title of the appeal) and of the address to which notices and other communications to the Secretary shall be sent;

(c) give notice to the appellant of the Board's address for service under these rules; and

(d) send to the appellant a copy of any representations in writing that the Board has submitted to the tribunal under rule 2 or rule 3.

Directions for further particulars

6.—(1) In any case in which an appellant has not sent to the Board further particulars in accordance with a notice sent by the Board under rule 3 the tribunal may, on the application of the Board (which may be sent to the Secretary with the documents referred to in rule 3(5)), by notice direct the appellant to supply such further particulars of the grounds on which he intends to rely and of any facts and contentions relevant thereto as may be specified in the notice, and the appellant shall send such particulars in duplicate to the Secretary within such time as the tribunal shall direct.

(2) Upon receipt of further particulars from the appellant the Secretary shall send a copy thereof to the Board.

(3) If the appellant makes default in complying with a direction made by the tribunal under this rule the tribunal may on the application of the Board dismiss the appeal or give such other directions as may seem proper.

(4) The tribunal may at any time by notice direct the Board to furnish any particulars relating to the assessment which appear to be requisite for the decision of the appeal, and thereupon the Board shall send the particulars to the Secretary and to the appellant.

Attendance of witnesses and discovery

7.—(1) On the application of the appellant or the Board made either by notice to the Secretary or at the hearing the tribunal may–

(a) grant to that party such discovery and inspection of documents as might be granted by a county court; or

(b) require any person (including a party) to attend as a witness and to give evidence or to produce any documents in his possession or power which relate to the appeal;

and may appoint the time at or within which or the place at which any act required in pursuance of this rule is to be done.

(2) A party on whom a requirement has been imposed under paragraph (1)(a) of this rule or a person on whom a requirement has been imposed under paragraph (1)(b) may, if such requirement was made upon an ex parte application, apply to the tribunal to vary or set aside the requirement, and notice of such an application shall be given to the party upon whose application the requirement was made.

(3) No application to vary or set aside a requirement as aforesaid shall be entertained by the tribunal in a case where a time has been appointed in relation to the requirement unless the application is made before the time or, as the case may be, the expiration of the time so appointed.

(4) Every document containing a requirement under paragraph (1) shall contain a reference to the fact that, under paragraph 1(7) of Schedule 9 to the 1978 Act, any person who without reasonable excuse fails to comply with any such requirement shall be liable on summary conviction to a fine, and the document shall state the amount of the current maximum fine.

Time and place of hearing of appeal

8. The President or a Regional Chairman shall fix the date, time and place of the hearing of an appeal, and the Secretary shall, not less than 14 days before the date so fixed, send to the appellant and to the Board a notice substantially in accordance with Form 2.

The hearing

9.—(1) Any hearing of an appeal shall be heard by a tribunal composed in accordance with section 128(2A), (2B) and (2C), or section 128(6), of the 1978 Act.

(2) Any hearing of or in connection with an appeal shall take place in public except where a Minister of the Crown has directed a tribunal to sit in private on grounds of national security in accordance with paragraph 1(4A) of Schedule 9 to the 1978 Act.

(3) Notwithstanding paragraph (2), a tribunal may sit in private for the purpose of–

(a) hearing evidence which in the opinion of the tribunal relates to matters of such a nature that it would be against the interests of national security to allow the evidence to be given in public; or

30

SCHEDULE 3—*continued*

> > (b) hearing evidence from any person which in the opinion of the tribunal is likely to consist of–
> >
> > > (i) information which he could not disclose without contravening a prohibition imposed by or under any enactment, or
> > >
> > > (ii) any information which has been communicated to him in confidence, or which he has otherwise obtained in consequence of the confidence reposed in him by another person, or
> > >
> > > (iii) information the disclosure of which would cause substantial injury to any undertaking of his or any undertaking in which he works for reasons other than its effect on negotiations with respect to any of the matters mentioned in section 244(1) of the 1992 Act.

(4) A member of the Council on Tribunals shall be entitled to attend any hearing taking place in private in his capacity as a member.

Procedure at hearing

10.—(1) At the hearing of an appeal the appellant and the Board shall be entitled to make opening statements, to call witnesses, to cross-examine any witnesses called by the other party and to address the tribunal.

(2) The appellant may if he so desires give evidence on his own behalf.

(3) If the appellant or the Board or both of them shall fail to appear or to be represented at the time and place fixed for a hearing the tribunal may dispose of the appeal or application in the absence of such party or parties or may adjourn the hearing to a later date: provided that before disposing of an appeal in the absence of either or both parties the tribunal shall consider any representations submitted by such party or parties under these rules.

(4) The tribunal may require any witnesses to give evidence on oath or affirmation in due form.

Decision of tribunal

11.—(1) Where a tribunal is composed of three members its decision may be taken by a majority; and if a tribunal is composed of two members only, the chairman shall have a second or casting vote.

(2) The decision of a tribunal shall be recorded in a document signed by the chairman which shall contain the reasons for the decision.

(3) The clerk shall transmit the document signed by the chairman to the Secretary who shall enter it in the Register, and shall send a copy of the entry to the appellant and the Board.

(4) The specification of the reasons for the decision shall be omitted from the Register in any case in which–

> (a) a Minister of the Crown has directed the tribunal, in accordance with paragraph 1(4A) of Schedule 9 to the 1978 Act, to sit in private on grounds of national security,
>
> (b) evidence has been heard in private and the tribunal so directs, or
>
> (c) the tribunal on the application of the appellant so directs on the ground that disclosure will be contrary to the interests of the appellant,

and in that event a specification of the reasons shall be sent to the appellant and the Board, and to any superior court in any proceedings relating to the decision, together with the copy of the entry.

(5) The chairman of the tribunal shall have power by certificate under his hand to correct in documents recording the tribunal's decisions clerical mistakes or errors arising therein from any accidental slip or omission.

(6) The clerk shall send a copy of any documents so corrected and the certificate of the chairman to the Secretary who shall thereupon make such correction as may be necessary in the Register and shall send a copy of the corrected entry or the corrected specification of the reasons, as the case may be, to the appellant and the Board.

Costs

12.—(1) The decision of the tribunal may include–

> (a) an order that the Board shall pay to the appellant or that the appellant shall pay to the Board either a specified sum in respect of the costs incurred by the appellant or the Board, as the case may be, or, in default of agreement, the taxed amount of those costs;
>
> (b) an order that the Board or the appellant shall pay to the Secretary of State the whole, or any part of, any allowances (other than allowances paid to members of tribunals) paid by the Secretary of State under paragraph 10 of Schedule 9 to the 1978 Act to any person, for

31

the purposes of, or in connection with, his attendance at the tribunal.

(2) Any costs required by an order under paragraph (1) to be taxed may be taxed in the county court according to such of the scales prescribed by county court rules for proceedings in the county court as shall be directed by the order.

Miscellaneous powers

13.—(1) The tribunal may if it thinks fit–

    (a) extend the time appointed by these rules for doing any act notwithstanding that the time appointed may have expired;

    (b) before granting an application referred to in rule 6(1), 6(3), 7(1) or 14, require the party making the application to give notice thereof to the other party;

    (c) postpone the day or time fixed for, or adjourn the hearing of, any appeal or application;

    (d) if at any time after the entry of the appeal in the Register the appellant gives notice of the abandonment of his appeal to the Secretary and to the Board, or the Board gives notice that the appeal is not contested to the Secretary and to the appellant, dismiss or allow the appeal, as the case may be, and thereupon rule 12 shall apply;

    (e) if the appellant and the Board agree in writing upon the terms of a decision to be made by the tribunal, decide accordingly.

(2) A notice under paragraph (1)(b) shall give particulars of the application and indicate the address to which and the time within which any objection to the application shall be made, being an address and time specified by the tribunal for the purposes of the application.

(3) Subject to the provisions of these rules the tribunal may regulate its own procedure.

(4) Any act required or authorised by these rules to be done by a tribunal may be done by a chairman except–

    (a) the hearing of an appeal under rule 9; and

    (b) an act required or authorised to be so done by rule 10 or 11 which the rule implies is to be done by the tribunal which is hearing or heard the appeal.

(5) Any functions of the Secretary other than those mentioned in rules 5 and 11 may be performed by a Regional Secretary.

Applications

14.—(1) An application to the tribunal for an extension of the time appointed by these rules for doing any act may be made by the appellant or the Board either before or (subject to rule 7(3)) after the expiration of the time so appointed.

(2) The appellant or the Board may at any time apply to the tribunal for directions on any matter arising in connection with an appeal.

(3) An application made under the foregoing provisions of these rules or to the tribunal for an extension of the time for appealing against an assessment to a levy shall be made by sending to the Secretary in duplicate a notice of application which shall state the time of the appeal, or the number of the assessment in the case where an appeal has not been entered in the Register, and shall set out the grounds of the application.

(4) The Secretary shall give notice to the appellant and to the Board of any extension of time granted by the tribunal or of any directions given by the tribunal in pursuance of these rules.

Notices, etc.

15.—(1) Any notice given under these rules shall be in writing, and all notices and documents required or authorised by these rules to be sent or given to any person hereinafter mentioned may be sent by post by means of the recorded delivery service or delivered to or at–

    (a) in the case of a notice of appeal, the Board's address for service specified in the assessment notice;

    (b) in the case of any other document directed to the Board, the Board's address for service;

    (c) in the case of a document (other than a notice of appeal) directed to the Secretary, the Office of the Tribunals or such other office as may be notified by the Secretary to the appellant and to the Board under rule 5(b) or paragraph (3);

    (d) in the case of a document directed to the appellant, his address for service specified in a notice given under these rules or, failing such a notice or if a notice sent to such an address has been returned, his last known address or place of business in the United Kingdom, or if the appellant is a corporation, such address or place of business or its registered or principal office;

32

SCHEDULE 3—*continued*

and if sent or given to the authorised representative of the appellant or the Board shall be deemed to have been sent or given to the appellant or the Board as the case may be.

(2) The appellant or the Board may at any time by notice to the Secretary and to the other party change his address for service under these rules.

(3) The Secretary shall give notice to the appellant and the Board of any change in an address of which notice has been given to the parties under rule 5(b).

33

SCHEDULE 3—*continued*

FORM 1

INDUSTRIAL TRAINING ACT 1982

NOTICE OF APPEAL AGAINST AN ASSESSMENT

TO

*INDUSTRIAL TRAINING BOARD

....[]

....

AND TO

The Secretary of the Tribunals (England and Wales)

I/We† .... of .... §
hereby give notice that I/we† appeal to an industrial tribunal under the Industrial Training Act
1982, section 12, against the assessment to the levy made by the above-mentioned industry training
board on .... 19.............................., being the
assessment numbered ....

Grounds of Appeal

The grounds of my/our† appeal are as follows:

Address for Service

All communications regarding the appeal should be addressed to me/us† at

....

to my/our● Solicitor(s)/Agent(s)●, Mr./Messrs.●

.... at§...

Date .... 19 ....

Signed .... ●

*   Insert name of the Board.
[]   Insert the address of the Board.
†   Delete if inapplicable.
§   Insert address applicable.
●   If the notice is signed on behalf of the appellant, the signatory must state in what capacity or
     what authority he signs.

34

FORM 2

INDUSTRIAL TRAINING ACT 1982

NOTICE OF HEARING

Case No ....   *Central/*Regional Office of the Industrial Tribunals (England and Wales),

Tribunal ....

       ....

NOTICE IS HEREBY GIVEN that the appeal of .... against the assessment to the levy made by the ....Industry Training Board and numbered .... will be heard by an industrial tribunal at .... on the .... day of .... at .... o'clock in the ....noon, or as soon as may be thereafter.

Unless the appellant receives from me a communication to the contrary, he should in his own interest appear at the hearing with his witnesses at the above time and place.

The appellant is entitled to be represented by counsel or solicitor or by another person.

If for any reason the appellant does not propose, or is unable, to appear at the hearing either in person or by representative, the appellant should immediately inform me in writing at the address mentioned at the head of this notice, stating the case number of the appeal and the reasons for the inability to attend or to be represented.

The appellant and the Board are entitled to submit representations in writing for consideration of the tribunal at the hearing of the appeal. Any such representations must be sent to the Secretary of the Industrial Tribunals (England and Wales) at the address mentioned at the head of this notice not less than seven days before the hearing, and a copy must be sent at the same time to the other party. If either or both parties fail to attend the hearing, the tribunal may dispose of the appeal in their absence, but in such case the tribunal will consider any representations so submitted.

       Dated .... 19 ....

       Signed ....
       *Secretary/*Regional Secretary

To the Appellant ....
       and

To ....Industry Training Board.

35

SCHEDULE 4 [Regulation 8(4)]

RULES OF PROCEDURE

APPLICABLE TO APPEALS AGAINST IMPROVEMENT AND PROHIBITION NOTICES

Notice of appeal

1. An appeal shall be commenced by the appellant sending to the Secretary a notice of appeal which shall be in writing and shall set out–

(a) the name and address of the appellant and, if different, an address within the United Kingdom to which he requires notices and documents relating to the appeal to be sent;

(b) the date of the improvement notice or prohibition notice appealed against and the address of the premises or place concerned;

(c) the name and address of the respondent;

(d) particulars of the requirements or directions appealed against; and

(e) the grounds of the appeal.

Time limit for bringing appeal

2.—(1) Subject to paragraph (2), the notice of appeal shall be sent to the Secretary within 21 days from the date of the service on the appellant of the notice appealed against.

(2) A tribunal may extend the time mentioned above where it is satisfied, on an application made in writing to the Secretary either before or after the expiration of that time, that it is not or was not reasonably practicable for an appeal to be brought within that time.

Action upon receipt of notice of appeal

3. Upon receiving a notice of appeal the Secretary shall enter particulars of it in the Register and shall send a copy of it to the respondent and inform the parties in writing of the case number of the appeal entered in the Register (which shall thereafter constitute the title of the proceedings) and of the address to which notices and other communications to the Secretary shall be sent.

Application for direction suspending the operation of a prohibition notice

4.—(1) Where an appeal has been brought against a prohibition notice and an application is made to the tribunal by the appellant in pursuance of section 24(3)(b) of the 1974 Act for a direction suspending the operation of the notice until the appeal is finally disposed of or withdrawn, the application shall be sent in writing to the Secretary and shall set out–

(a) the case number of the appeal if known to the appellant or particulars sufficient to identify the appeal; and

(b) the grounds on which the application is made.

(2) Upon receiving the application, the Secretary shall enter particulars of it against the entry in the Register relating to the appeal and shall send a copy of it to the respondent.

Power to require attendance of witnesses and production of documents, etc.

5.—(1) A tribunal may on the application of a party made either by notice to the Secretary or at the hearing–

(a) require a party to furnish in writing to another party further particulars of the grounds on which he relies and of any facts and contentions relevant thereto;

(b) grant to a party such discovery or inspection of documents as might be granted by a county court; and

(c) require the attendance of any person as a witness or require the production of any document relating to the matter to be determined,

and may appoint the time at or within which or the place at which any act required in pursuance of this rule is to be done.

(2) The tribunal shall not under paragraph (1) require the production of any document certified by the Secretary of State as being a document of which the production would be against the interests of national security.

(3) A person on whom a requirement has been made under paragraph (1) may apply to the tribunal either by notice to the Secretary or at the hearing to vary or set aside the requirement.

(4) No such application to vary or set aside shall be entertained in a case where a time has been appointed under paragraph (1) in relation to the requirement unless it is made before the time or, as the case may be, expiration on the time so appointed.

SCHEDULE 4—*continued*

(5) Every document containing a requirement under paragraph (1)(b) or (c) shall contain a reference to the fact that under paragraph 1(7) of Schedule 9 to the 1978 Act any person who without reasonable excuse fails to comply with any such requirement shall be liable on summary conviction to a fine, and the document shall state the amount of the current maximum fine.

Time and place of hearing and appointment of assessor

6.—(1) The President or a Regional Chairman shall fix the date, time and place of the hearing of the appeal and the Secretary shall not less than 14 days (or such shorter time as may be agreed by him with the parties) before the date so fixed send to each party a notice of hearing together with information and guidance as to attendance at the hearing, witnesses and the bringing of documents (if any), representation by another person and written representations.

(2) Where the President or a Regional Chairman so directs, the Secretary shall also send notice of the hearing to such persons as may be directed, but the requirement as to the period of notice contained in paragraph (1) shall not apply to any such notice.

(3) The President or a Regional Chairman may, if he thinks fit, appoint in pursuance of section 24(4) of the 1974 Act a person or persons having special knowledge or experience in relation to the subject matter of the appeal to sit with the tribunal as assessor or assessors.

The hearing

7.—(1) Any hearing of an appeal shall be heard by a tribunal composed in accordance with section 128(2A), (2B) and (2C), or section 128(6), of the 1978 Act.

(2) Any hearing of or in connection with an appeal shall take place in public except where a Minister of the Crown has directed a tribunal to sit in private on grounds of national security in accordance with paragraph 1(4A) of Schedule 9 to the 1978 Act.

(3) Notwithstanding paragraph (2), a tribunal may sit in private, if on the application of a party the tribunal considers it appropriate to do so, for the purpose of hearing evidence–

(a) which relates to matters of such a nature that it would be against the interests of national security to allow the evidence to be given in public, or

(b) hearing evidence from any person which in the opinion of the tribunal is likely to consist of information the disclosure of which would cause substantial injury to the undertaking of the appellant or of any undertaking in which he works for reasons other than its effect on negotiations with respect to any of the matters mentioned in section 244(1) of the 1992 Act.

(4) A member of the Council on Tribunals shall be entitled to attend any hearing in his capacity as a member.

Written representations

8. If a party wishes to submit representations in writing for consideration by a tribunal at the hearing of the appeal, that party shall present his representations to the Secretary not less than 7 days before the hearing and shall at the same time send a copy of it to the other party.

Procedure at hearing

9.—(1) At any hearing of or in connection with an appeal a party shall be entitled to make an opening statement, to give evidence on his own behalf, to call witnesses, to cross-examine any witnesses called by the other party and to address the tribunal.

(2) If a party shall fail to appear or to be represented at the time and place fixed for the hearing of an appeal, the tribunal may dispose of the appeal in the absence of that party or may adjourn the hearing to a later date: provided that before disposing of an appeal in the absence of a party the tribunal shall consider any written representations submitted by that party in pursuance of rule 8.

(3) A tribunal may require any witness to give evidence on oath or affirmation and for that purpose there may be administered an oath or affirmation in due form.

Decision of tribunal

10.—(1) Where a tribunal is composed of three members its decision may be taken by a majority; and if a tribunal is composed of two members only, the chairman shall have a second or casting vote.

(2) The decision of a tribunal shall be recorded in a document signed by the chairman which shall contain the reasons for the decision.

37

(3) The clerk shall transmit the document signed by the chairman to the Secretary who shall enter it in the Register and shall send a copy of the entry to each of the parties.

(4) The specification of the reasons for the decision shall be omitted from the Register in any case in which–

    (a) a Minister of the Crown has directed the tribunal, in accordance with paragraph 1(4A) of Schedule 9 to the 1978 Act, to sit in private on grounds of national security, or

    (b) evidence has been heard in private and the tribunal so directs,

and in that event a specification of the reasons shall be sent to the parties and to any superior court in any proceedings relating to such decision together with the copy of the entry.

(5) The chairman of a tribunal shall have power by certificate under his hand to correct in documents recording the tribunal's decisions clerical mistakes or errors arising therein from any accidental slip or omission.

(6) The clerk shall send a copy of any document so corrected and the certificate of the chairman to the Secretary who shall as soon as practicable make such correction as may be necessary in the Register and shall send a copy of the corrected entry or of the corrected specification of the reasons, as the case may be, to each of the parties.

(7) If any decision is–

    (a) corrected under paragraph (5),

    (b) reviewed, revoked or varied under rule 11, or

    (c) altered in any way by order of a superior court,

the Secretary shall alter the entry in the Register to conform with any such certificate or order and shall send a copy of the new entry to each of the parties.

Review of tribunal's decision

11.—(1) A tribunal shall have power on the application of a party to review and revoke or vary by certificate under the chairman's hand any of its decisions on the grounds that–

    (a) the decision was wrongly made as a result of an error on the part of the tribunal staff;

    (b) a party did not receive notice of the proceedings leading to the decision;

    (c) the decision was made in the absence of a party;

    (d) new evidence has become available since the making of the decision provided that its existence could not have been reasonably known of or foreseen; or

    (e) the interests of justice require such a review.

(2) An application for the purposes of paragraph (1) may be made at the hearing. If the application is not made at the hearing, such application shall be made to the Secretary within 14 days from the date of the entry of a decision in the Register and must be in writing stating the grounds in full.

(3) An application for the purposes of paragraph (1) may be refused by the chairman of the tribunal which decided the case, by the President or by a Regional Chairman if in his opinion it has no reasonable prospect of success and he shall state the reasons for his opinion.

(4) If such an application is not refused under paragraph (3), it shall be heard by the tribunal and if it is granted the tribunal shall either vary its decision or revoke its decision and order a re-hearing.

(5) The clerk shall send to the Secretary the certificate of the chairman as to any revocation or variation of the tribunal's decision under this rule. The Secretary shall as soon as practicable make such correction as may be necessary in the Register and shall send a copy of the entry to each of the parties.

Costs

12.—(1) A tribunal may make an order that a party shall pay to another party either a specified sum in respect of the costs of or in connection with an appeal incurred by that other party or, in default of agreement, the taxed amount of those costs.

(2) Any costs required by an order under this rule to be taxed may be taxed in the county court according to such of the scales prescribed by the county court rules for proceedings in the county court as shall be directed by the order.

Miscellaneous powers

13.—(1) Subject to the provisions of these rules, a tribunal may regulate its own procedure.

(2) A tribunal may, if it thinks fit–

    (a) postpone the day or time fixed for, or adjourn, any hearing;

    (b) before granting an application under rule 5 or 11 require the party making the application to give notice thereof to the other party;

    (c) either on the application of any person or of its own motion, direct any other person to be joined as a party to the appeal (giving such consequential directions as it considers necessary), but may do so only after having given to the person proposed to be joined a reasonable opportunity of making written or oral objection;

    (d) make any necessary amendments to the description of a party in the Register and in other documents relating to the appeal;

    (e) if the appellant shall at any time give notice of the abandonment of his appeal, dismiss the appeal;

    (f) if the parties agree in writing upon the terms of a decision to be made by the tribunal, decide accordingly.

(3) Any act required or authorised by these rules to be done by a tribunal may be done by a chairman except–

    (a) the hearing of an appeal under rule 8;

    (b) an act required or authorised to be so done by rule 9 or 10 which the rule implies is to be done by the tribunal which is hearing or heard the appeal;

    (c) the hearing of an application under rule 11(1), and the variation or revocation of a decision, and ordering of a re-hearing, under rule 11(4);

    (d) the granting of an extension of time under rule 2(2).

(4) Any function of the Secretary may be performed by a Regional Secretary.

Notices, etc.

14.—(1) Any notice given under these rules shall be in writing and all notices and documents required or authorised by these rules to be sent or given to any person hereinafter mentioned may be sent by post (subject to paragraphs (3) and (4)) or delivered to or at–

    (a) in the case of a document directed to the Secretary, the Office of the Tribunals or such other office as may be notified by the Secretary to the parties;

    (b) in the case of a document directed to a party, his address for service specified in the notice of appeal or in a notice under paragraph (2) or (if no address for service is so specified or if a notice sent to such an address has been returned), his last known address or place of business in the United Kingdom or, if the party is a corporation, the corporation's registered or principal office;

    (c) in the case of a document directed to any person (other than a person specified in the foregoing provisions of this paragraph), his address or place of business in the United Kingdom, or if such a person is a corporation, the corporation's registered or principal office;

and if sent or given to the authorised representative of a party shall be deemed to have been sent or given to that party.

(2) A party may at any time by notice to the Secretary and to the other party change his address for service under these rules.

(3) Where a notice of appeal is not delivered, it shall be sent by the recorded delivery service.

(4) Where for any sufficient reason service of any document or notice cannot be effected in the manner prescribed under this rule, the President or a Regional Chairman may make an order for substituted service in such manner as he may deem fit and such service shall have the same effect as service in the manner prescribed under this rule.

(5) In the case of an appeal to which the respondent is an inspector appointed otherwise than by the Health and Safety Executive, the Secretary shall send to that executive copies of the notice of appeal and the document recording the decision of the tribunal on the appeal.

39

RULES OF PROCEDURE

APPLICABLE TO APPEALS AGAINST NON-DISCRIMINATION NOTICES

Notice of appeal

1. An appeal shall be commenced not later than six weeks after service of the non-discrimination notice, as specified in section 68(1) of the 1975 Act and in section 59(1) of the 1976 Act, by the appellant sending to the Secretary a notice of appeal which shall be in writing and shall set out–

    (a) the name and address of the appellant and, if different, an address within the United Kingdom to which he requires notices and documents relating to the appeal to be sent;

    (b) the date of the non-discrimination notice appealed against;

    (c) the name and address of the respondent;

    (d) particulars of the requirements appealed against; and

    (e) the grounds of the appeal.

Action upon receipt of notice of appeal

2. Upon receiving a notice of appeal the Secretary shall, subject to rule 11(3), enter particulars of it in the Register and shall send a copy of it to the respondent and inform the parties in writing of the case number of the appeal entered in the Register (which shall thereafter constitute the title of the proceedings) and of the address to which notices and other communications to the Secretary shall be sent.

Power to require attendance of witnesses and production of documents, etc.

3.—(1) A tribunal may on the application of a party made either by notice to the Secretary or at the hearing–

    (a) require a party to furnish in writing to another party further particulars of the grounds on which he relies and of any facts and contentions relevant thereto;

    (b) grant to a party such discovery or inspection of documents as might be granted by a county court; and

    (c) require the attendance of any person as a witness or require the production of any document relating to the matter to be determined,

and may appoint the time at or within which or the place at which any act required in pursuance of this rule is to be done.

(2) The tribunal shall not under paragraph (1) require the production of any document certified by the Secretary of State as being a document of which the production would be against the interests of national security.

(3) A person on whom a requirement has been made under paragraph (1) may apply to the tribunal either by notice to the Secretary or at the hearing to vary or set aside the requirement.

(4) No such application to vary or set aside shall be entertained in a case where a time has been appointed under paragraph (1) in relation to the requirement unless it is made before the time or, as the case may be, expiration of the time so appointed.

(5) Every document containing a requirement under paragraph (1)(b) or (c) shall contain a reference to the fact that, under paragraph 1(7) of Schedule 9 to the 1978 Act, any person who without reasonable excuse fails to comply with any such requirement shall be liable on summary conviction to a fine, and the document shall state the amount of the current maximum fine.

Time and place of hearing

4.—(1) The President or a Regional Chairman shall fix the date, time and place of the hearing of the appeal and the Secretary shall not less than 14 days (or such shorter time as may be agreed by him with the parties) before the date so fixed send to each party a notice of hearing together with information and guidance as to attendance at the hearing, witnesses and the bringing of documents (if any), representation by another person and written representations.

(2) Where the President or a Regional Chairman so directs, the Secretary shall also send notice of the hearing to such persons as may be directed, but the requirements as to the period of notice contained in paragraph (1) shall not apply to any such notices.

SCHEDULE 5—*continued*

The hearing

5.—(1) Any hearing of an appeal shall be heard by a tribunal composed in accordance with section 128(2A), (2B) and (2C), or section 128(6), of the 1978 Act.

(2) Any hearing of or in connection with an appeal shall take place in public except where a Minister of the Crown has directed a tribunal to sit in private on grounds of national security in accordance with paragraph 1(4A) of Schedule 9 to the 1978 Act.

(3) Notwithstanding paragraph (2), a tribunal may sit in private, if on the application of a party the tribunal considers it appropriate to do so, for the purpose of hearing evidence–

(a) which relates to matters of such a nature that it would be against the interests of national security to allow the evidence to be given in public, or

(b) hearing evidence from any person which in the opinion of the tribunal is likely to consist of information the disclosure of which would cause substantial injury to the undertaking of the appellant or of any undertaking in which he works for reasons other than its effect on negotiations with respect to any of the matters mentioned in section 244(1) of the 1992 Act.

(4) A member of the Council on Tribunals shall be entitled to attend any hearing in his capacity as a member.

Written representations

6. If a party wishes to submit representations in writing for consideration by a tribunal at the hearing of the appeal, that party shall send such representations to the Secretary not less than 7 days before the hearing and shall at the same time send a copy thereof to the other party.

Procedure at hearing

7.—(1) At any hearing of or in connection with an appeal a party shall be entitled to make an opening statement, to give evidence, to call witnesses, to cross-examine any witnesses called by the other party and to address the tribunal.

(2) If a party shall fail to appear or to be represented at the time and place fixed for the hearing of an appeal, the tribunal may dispose of the appeal in the absence of that party or may adjourn the hearing to a later date: provided that before disposing of an appeal in the absence of a party the tribunal shall consider any written representations submitted by that party in pursuance of rule 6.

(3) A tribunal may require any witness to give evidence on oath or affirmation and for that purpose there may be administered an oath or affirmation in due form.

Decision of tribunal

8.—(1) Where a tribunal is composed of three members its decision may be taken by a majority; and if a tribunal is composed of two members only, the chairman shall have a second or casting vote.

(2) The decision of a tribunal shall be recorded in a document signed by the chairman which shall contain the reasons for the decision.

(3) The clerk shall transmit the document signed by the chairman to the Secretary who shall enter it in the Register and shall send a copy of the entry to each of the parties.

(4) The specification of the reasons for the decision shall be omitted from the Register in any case in which–

(a) a Minister of the Crown has directed the tribunal, in accordance with paragraph 1 (4A) of Schedule 9 to the 1978 Act, to sit in private on grounds of national security, or

(b) evidence has been heard in private and the tribunal so directs,

and in that event a specification of the reasons shall be sent to the parties and to any superior court in any proceedings relating to such decision together with the copy of the entry.

(5) In any appeal appearing to involve allegations of a sexual offence, the document referred to in paragraph (3) shall be entered on the Register with such deletions or amendments as have been made in accordance with rule 11(3).

(6) The chairman shall have power by certificate under his hand to correct in documents recording the tribunal's decisions clerical mistakes or errors arising therein from any accidental slip or omission.

(7) The clerk shall send a copy of any document so corrected and the certificate of the chairman to the Secretary who shall as soon as practicable make such corrections as may be necessary in the

41

SCHEDULE 5—*continued*

Register and shall send a copy of the corrected entry or of the corrected specification of the reasons, as the case may be, to each of the parties.

(8) If any decision is–

    (a) corrected under paragraph (6),

    (b) reviewed, revoked or varied under rule 9, or

    (c) altered in any way by order of a superior court,

the Secretary shall alter the entry in the Register to conform with any such certificate or order and shall send a copy of the new entry to each of the parties.

Review of tribunal's decision

9.—(1) A tribunal shall have power on the application of a party to review and to revoke or vary by certificate under the chairman's hand any of its decisions on the grounds that–

    (a) the decision was wrongly made as a result of an error on the part of the tribunal staff;

    (b) a party did not receive notice of the proceedings leading to the decision;

    (c) the decision was made in the absence of a party;

    (d) new evidence has become available since the making of the decision provided that its existence could not have been reasonably known of or foreseen; or

    (e) the interests of justice require such a review.

(2) An application for the purposes of paragraph (1) may be made at the hearing. If the application is not made at the hearing, such application shall be made to the Secretary at any time from the date of the hearing until 14 days after the date on which the decision was sent to the parties and must be in writing stating the grounds in full.

(3) An application for the purposes of paragraph (1) may be refused by the chairman of the tribunal which decided the case, by the President or by a Regional Chairman if in his opinion it has no reasonable prospect of success and he shall state the reasons for his opinion.

(4) If such an application is not refused under paragraph (3), it shall be heard by the tribunal and if it is granted the tribunal shall either vary its decision or revoke its decision and order a re-hearing.

(5) The clerk shall send to the Secretary the certificate of the chairman as to any revocation or variation of the tribunal's decision under this rule. The Secretary shall as soon as practicable make such correction as may be necessary in the Register and shall send a copy of the entry to each of the parties.

Costs

10.—(1) A tribunal may make an order that a party shall pay to another party either a specified sum in respect of the costs of or in connection with an appeal incurred by that other party or, in default of agreement, the taxed amount of those costs.

(2) Any costs required by an order under this rule to be taxed may be taxed in the county court according to such of the scales prescribed by the county court rules for proceedings in the county court as shall be directed by the order.

Miscellaneous powers

11.—(1) Subject to the provisions of these rules, a tribunal may regulate its own procedure.

(2) A tribunal may–

    (a) postpone the day or time fixed for, or adjourn, any hearing;

    (b) before granting an application under rule 3 or 9 require the party making the application to give notice thereof to the other party;

    (c) either on the application of any person or of its own motion, direct any other person to be joined as a party to the appeal (giving such consequential directions as it considers necessary), but may do so only after having given to the person proposed to be joined a reasonable opportunity of making written or oral objection;

    (d) make any necessary amendments to the description of a party in the Register and in other documents relating to the appeal;

    (e) if the appellant shall at any time give notice of the abandonment of his appeal, dismiss the appeal;

    (f) if the parties agree in writing upon the terms of a decision to be made by the tribunal, decide accordingly.

42

SCHEDULE 5—*continued*

(3) In any appeal appearing to involve allegations of the commission of a sexual offence, the tribunal or the Secretary shall omit from the Register, or delete from the Register or any decision, document or record of the proceedings, which is available to the public, any identifying matter which is likely to lead members of the public to identify any person affected by or making such an allegation.

(4) Any act required or authorised by these rules to be done by a tribunal may be done by a chairman except–

(a) the hearing of an appeal under rule 5;

(b) an act required or authorised to be so done by rule 7 or 8 which the rule implies is to be done by the tribunal which is hearing or has heard the appeal;

(c) the hearing of an application under rule 9(1), and the variation or revocation of a decision, and ordering of a re-hearing, under rule 9(4).

(5) Any functions of the Secretary may be performed by a Regional Secretary.

Restricted reporting orders

12.—(1) In any appeal which involves allegations of sexual misconduct the tribunal may at any time before promulgation of its decision, either on the application of a party made by notice to the Secretary or of its own motion, make a restricted reporting order.

(2) The tribunal shall not make a restricted reporting order unless it has given each party an opportunity to advance oral argument at a hearing, if they so wish.

(3) Where a tribunal makes a restricted reporting order–

(a) it shall specify in the order the persons who may not be identified;

(b) the order shall remain in force until the promulgation of the decision of the tribunal on the appeal to which it relates unless revoked earlier; and

(c) the Regional Secretary shall ensure that a notice of that fact is displayed on the notice board of the tribunal with any list of the proceedings taking place before the industrial tribunal, and on the door of the room in which the proceedings affected by the order are taking place.

(4) A tribunal may revoke a restricted reporting order at any time if it thinks fit.

(5) For the purposes of this rule "promulgation" occurs on the date recorded as being the date on which the document recording the determination of the appeal was sent to the parties.

Notices, etc.

13.—(1) Any notice given under these rules shall be in writing and all notices and documents required or authorised by these rules to be sent or given to any person hereinafter mentioned may be sent by post (subject to paragraphs (3) and (4)) or delivered to or at–

(a) in the case of a document directed to the Secretary, the Office of the Tribunals or such other office as may be notified by the Secretary to the parties;

(b) in the case of a document directed to a party, his address for service specified in the notice of appeal or in a notice under paragraph (2) or (if no address for service is so specified or if a notice sent to such an address has been returned), his last known address or place of business in the United Kingdom, or if the party is a corporation, the corporation's registered or principal office;

(c) in the case of a document directed to any person (other than a person specified in the foregoing provisions of this paragraph), his address or place of business in the United Kingdom, or if such a person is a corporation, the corporation's registered or principal office;

and if sent or given to the authorised representative of a party shall be deemed to have been sent or given to that party.

(2) A party may at any time by notice to the Secretary and to the other party change his address for service under these rules.

(3) Where a notice of appeal is not delivered, it shall be sent by the recorded delivery service.

(4) Where for any sufficient reason service of any document or notice cannot be effected in the manner prescribed under this rule, the President or a Regional Chairman may make an order for substituted service in such manner as he may deem fit and such service shall have the same effect as service in the manner prescribed under this rule.

43

EXPLANATORY NOTE

(This note is not part of the Regulations)

These Regulations, which come into force on 16th December 1993, replace the regulations which establish industrial tribunals. The Regulations contain, in Schedules 1 to 5, new rules of procedure for proceedings before industrial tribunals which replace the existing rules of procedure. The Regulations apply to proceedings in England and Wales.

The rules in the Schedules apply to the following proceedings–

Schedule 1 — all proceedings other than those to which Schedules 3, 4 and 5 apply or to which separate rules of procedure made under any enactment apply,

Schedule 2 — proceedings involving a claim for equal pay for work of equal value under the Equal Pay Act 1970 (the rules in Schedule 2 are complementary to those in Schedule 1 which also applies to these proceedings);

Schedule 3 — appeals against assessments to industrial training levy under levy orders made under the Industrial Training Act 1982;

Schedule 4 — appeals against improvement notices and prohibition notices served under the Health and Safety at Work etc. Act 1974;

Schedule 5 — appeals against non-discrimination notices served under the Sex Discrimination Act 1975 or the Race Relations Act 1976.

The Regulations and rules incorporate provisions which implement or take account of the following recent provisions of primary legislation–

(a) sections 128(2A), (2B), (2C), (2D), (2E) and (2F) of the Employment Protection (Consolidation) Act 1978 ("the 1978 Act"), inserted by sections 36(1) and (2) of the Trade Union Reform and Employment Rights Act 1993 ("the 1993 Act"), which specify when a tribunal is to consist of three persons and when it is to consist of only a chairman;

(b) section 128(6) of the 1978 Act, inserted by sections 36(1) and (3) of the 1993 Act, which enables a Minister of the Crown, on grounds of national security, to direct tribunal proceedings to be heard and determined by the President of Industrial Tribunals (England and Wales);

(c) paragraph 1(4A) of Schedule 9 to the 1978 Act ("Schedule 9"), inserted by paragraph 6(a) of Schedule 7 to the 1993 Act, which enables a Minister of the Crown, on grounds of national security, to direct a tribunal to sit in private;

(d) paragraph 1(5A) of Schedule 9, inserted by section 40 of the 1993 Act (restriction of publicity in cases involving sexual misconduct);

(e) paragraph 1A of Schedule 9, inserted by section 20 of the Employment Act 1989 (c.38), which enables regulations to provide for tribunals to carry out pre-hearing reviews and, on such a review, to require a party to pay a deposit not exceeding £150 as a condition of the party continuing to participate in the proceedings; and

(f) paragraph 1B of Schedule 9, inserted by paragraph 28(c) of Schedule 8 to the 1993 Act, which enables regulations to provide for tribunals to hear and determine issues relating to the entitlement of parties to contest the proceedings before hearing and determining the proceedings as a whole.

In addition, the rules have been modernised and amended to introduce a number of improvements to the procedures contained in the superseded rules.

The Regulations and rules will apply to all proceedings before industrial tribunals as from 16th December 1993, whenever the proceedings were commenced.

The Regulations contain transitional provisions.

STATUTORY INSTRUMENTS

1994 No. 1623

INDUSTRIAL TRIBUNALS

The Industrial Tribunals Extension of Jurisdiction (England and Wales) Order 1994

Made - - - -	*11th July 1994*
Coming into force	*12th July 1994*

Whereas a draft of the following Order was laid before Parliament in accordance with section 131(8) of the Employment Protection (Consolidation) Act 1978 (**a**) and approved by resolution of each House of Parliament.

Now, therefore, the Lord Chancellor, in exercise of the powers conferred on him by sections 131(1), (4A), (5) and (5A) and 154(3) of that Act (**b**), and of all other powers enabling him in that behalf, hereby makes the following Order:–

Citation, commencement and interpretation

1.—(1) This Order may be cited as the Industrial Tribunals Extension of Jurisdiction (England and Wales) Order 1994 and comes into force on the first day after it is made.

(2) In this Order–

"contract claim" means a claim in respect of which proceedings may be brought before an industrial tribunal by virtue of article 3 or 4; and

"the 1978 Act" means the Employment Protection (Consolidation) Act 1978.

Transitional provision

2. This Order does not enable proceedings in respect of a contract claim to be brought before an industrial tribunal unless–

(a) the effective date of termination (as defined in section 55(4) of the 1978 Act) in respect of the contract giving rise to the claim, or

(b) where there is no effective date of termination, the last day upon which the employee works in the employment which has terminated,

occurs on or after the day on which the Order comes into force.

Extension of jurisdiction

3. Proceedings may be brought before an industrial tribunal in respect of a claim of an employee for the recovery of damages or any other sum (other than a claim for damages, or for a sum due, in respect of personal injuries) if–

(a) the claim is one to which section 131(2) of the 1978 Act applies and which a court in England and Wales would under the law for the time being in force have jurisdiction to hear and determine;

(b) the claim is not one to which article 5 applies; and

(**a**) 1978 c.44; section 131 was amended by section 38 of the Trade Union Reform and Employment Rights Act 1993 (c.19).

(**b**) By virtue of section 131(1), the power to make this Order is vested in "the appropriate Minister" which expression is defined in section 131(7) to mean, as respects a claim in respect of which an action could be heard and determined in England and Wales, the Lord Chancellor.

(c) the claim arises or is outstanding on the termination of the employee's employment.

4. Proceedings may be brought before an industrial tribunal in respect of a claim of an employer for the recovery of damages or any other sum (other than a claim for damages, or for a sum due, in respect of personal injuries) if–

    (a) the claim is one to which section 131(2) of the 1978 Act applies and which a court in England and Wales would under the law for the time being in force have jurisdiction to hear and determine;

    (b) the claim is not one to which article 5 applies;

    (c) the claim arises or is outstanding on the termination of the employment of the employee against whom it is made; and

    (d) proceedings in respect of a claim of that employee have been brought before an industrial tribunal by virtue of this Order.

5. This article applies to a claim for breach of a contractual term of any of the following descriptions–

    (a) a term requiring the employer to provide living accommodation for the employee;

    (b) a term imposing an obligation on the employer or the employee in connection with the provision of living accommodation;

    (c) a term relating to intellectual property;

    (d) a term imposing an obligation of confidence;

    (e) a term which is a covenant in restraint of trade.

In this article, "intellectual property" includes copyright, rights in performances, moral rights, design right, registered designs, patents and trade marks.

Manner in which proceedings may be brought

6. Proceedings on a contract claim may be brought before an industrial tribunal by presenting a complaint to an industrial tribunal.

Time within which proceedings may be brought

7. An industrial tribunal shall not entertain a complaint in respect of an employee's contract claim unless it is presented–

    (a) within the period of three months beginning with the effective date of termination of the contract giving rise to the claim, or

    (b) where there is no effective date of termination, within the period of three months beginning with the last day upon which the employee worked in the employment which has terminated, or

    (c) where the tribunal is satisfied that it was not reasonably practicable for the complaint to be presented within whichever of those periods is applicable, within such further period as the tribunal considers reasonable.

8. An industrial tribunal shall not entertain a complaint in respect of an employer's contract claim unless–

    (a) it is presented at a time when there is before the tribunal a complaint in respect of a contract claim of a particular employee which has not been settled or withdrawn;

    (b) it arises out of a contract with that employee; and

    (c) it is presented–

        (i) within the period of six weeks beginning with the day, or if more than one the last of the days, on which the employer (or other person who is the respondent party to the employee's contract claim) received from the tribunal a copy of an originating application in respect of a contract claim of that employee; or

2

(ii) where the tribunal is satisfied that it was not reasonably practicable for the complaint to be presented within that period, within such further period as the tribunal considers reasonable.

Death and bankruptcy

9.—(1) Where proceedings in respect of a contract claim have been brought before an industrial tribunal and an employee or employer party to them dies before their conclusion, the proceedings shall not abate by reason of the death and the tribunal may, if it thinks it necessary in order to ensure that all matters in dispute may be effectually and completely determined and adjudicated upon, order the personal representatives of the deceased party, or other persons whom the tribunal considers appropriate, to be made parties and the proceedings to be carried on as if they had been substituted for the deceased party.

(2) Where proceedings in respect of a contract claim have been brought before an industrial tribunal and the employee or employer who is the applicant party to them becomes bankrupt before their conclusion, the proceedings shall not abate by reason of the bankruptcy and the tribunal may, if it thinks it necessary in order to ensure that all matters in dispute may be effectually and completely adjudicated upon, order the person in whom the interest of the bankrupt party has vested to be made a party and the proceedings to be carried on as if he had been substituted for the bankrupt party.

Limit on payment to be ordered

10. An industrial tribunal shall not in proceedings in respect of a contract claim, or in respect of a number of contract claims relating to the same contract, order the payment of an amount exceeding £25,000.

Dated 11th July 1994 *Mackay of Clashfern, C.*

3

EXPLANATORY NOTE

(This note is not part of the Order)

This Order, which applies in relation to England and Wales and comes into force on the day after it is made, enables an employee to bring a claim for damages for breach of his contract of employment, or for a sum due under that contract, before an industrial tribunal if the claim arises or is outstanding on the termination of his employment. The Order also enables an employer to make such a claim against an employee where the employee has claimed against him under the Order.

Article 5 contains certain exclusions. Broadly, these relate to claims about the provision of living accommodation, intellectual property (for example, copyright), obligations of confidence on the employee and covenants in restraint of trade.

Articles 7 and 8 provide that an employee's complaint about a contractual claim must normally be presented within a period of three months beginning with the "effective date of termination" as defined in section 55(4) of the Employment Protection (Consolidation) Act 1978, and that an employer's complaint about a contractual claim must be presented within six weeks of receiving a copy of an originating application relating to the employee's complaint. The tribunal is given a discretion to allow a complaint to be presented later if it was not reasonably practicable for the complaint to be presented within these periods.

Article 10 provides that the maximum which a tribunal may order to be paid in respect of a contract claim, or a number of claims relating to the same contract, is £25,000.

The Order contains a transitional provision.

ISBN 0-11-044623-2

Printed in the United Kingdom for HMSO
795/WO 1578 C12 7/94 547/2 9385/2119/0161 272070

9 780110 446233

Sex Discrimination Act 1975 Section 74 (1)(a)

Questionnaire of person aggrieved (The Complainant)

Name of person to be questioned (the respondent)	To:
Address	Of:
Name of complainant	1.
Address	Of:
	Consider that you may have discriminated against me contrary to the Sex Discrimination Act 1975.
Give date, approximate time, place and factual description of the treatment received and of the circumstances leading up to the treatment (see paragraph 9 of the guidance)	2. On
Complete if you wish to give reasons, otherwise delete the word 'because' (see paragraphs 10 and 11 of the guidance)	3. I consider that this treatment may have been unlawful because
This is the first of your questions to the Respondent. You are advised not to alter it	4. Do you agree that the statement in paragraph 2 is an accurate description of what happened? If not in what respect do you disagree or what is your version of what happened?

This is the second of your questions to the Respondent. You are advised not to alter it	5. Do you accept that your treatment of me was unlawful discrimination by you against me? If not a) Why not? b) For what reason did I receive the treatment accorded to me? c) How far did my sex or marital status affect your treatment of me?
Enter here any other questions you wish to ask (see paragraphs 12–14 of the guidance)	6.
* Delete as appropriate. If you delete the first alternative, insert the address to which you want the reply to be sent	7. My address for any reply you may wish to give to the questions raised above is * that set out in paragraph 1 above/the following address
See paragraph 15 of the guidance	Signature of complainant .... Date ....

N.B. *By virtue of Section 74 of the Act, this questionnaire and any reply are (subject to the provisions of the section) admissible in proceedings under the Act and a court or tribunal may draw any such inference as is just and equitable from a failure without reasonable excuse to reply within a reasonable period, or from an evasive or equivocal reply, including an inference that the person questioned has discriminated unlawfully.*

Sex Discrimination Act 1975 Section 74 (1)(b)

Reply: The Respondent

Note: Before completing this reply form, we advise you to prepare what you want to say on a separate piece of paper. If you have insufficient room on the reply form for what you want to say, continue on an additional piece of paper, which should be attached to the reply form and sent to the Complainant.

Enter the name of the person you are reply to (the Complainant).	To:
Enter the Complainant's address.	Of:
Enter your name (you are the Respondent).	1.
Enter your address.	Of:
Complete as necessary.	Hereby acknowledge receipt of the questionnaire signed by you and dated: / which was served on me on
Please tick relevant box: you are answering question 4 of the Complainant's statement of event, you should explain in what respects you disagree, or your version of what happened, or both.	2. I agree/disagree that the statement in paragraph 2 of the questionnaire is an inaccurate description of what happened. I disagree with the statement in paragraph 2 of the questionnaire in that:

3. I accept/dispute that my treatment of you was unlawful discrimination by me against you.

3a. My reasons for so disputing are:

3b. The reason why you received the treatment accorded to you is:

3c. Your sex or marital status affected my treatment of you to the following extent:

Replies to the questions in paragraph 6 of the Complainant's questionnaire can be entered here.

4.

Delete the whole of this sentence if you have answered all the questions asked in the Complainant's questionnaire. If you are unable or unwilling to answer the questions please delete as appropriate and give your reasons for not answering them.

5. I have deleted (in whole or in part) the paragraph(s) numbered above since I am unable/unwilling to reply to the relevant questions of the questionnaire for the following reasons:

The reply form must be signed and dated. If it is to be signed on behalf of (rather than by) the Respondent the person signing should:

- Describe himself/herself e.g., 'Solicitor acting for (name of Respondent)'; or 'Personnel Manager of (name of firm)'; and

- Give business address (or home address if appropriate).

Signature of the Respondent ....

Dated ....

How to serve the reply form on the Complainant

- If you wish to reply to the questionnaire we strongly advise that you do so without delay.
- You should retain and keep in a safe place the questionnaire sent to you and a copy of your reply.
- You can serve the reply either by delivering it in person to the Complainant or by sending it by post.
- If you send it by post, we advise you to use the recorded delivery service (*this will provide you with evidence of delivery*).
- You should send the reply form to the address indicated in paragraph 7 of the Complainant's questionnaire.

Disability Discrimination Act 1995 S 56 (2)(A)

Questionnaire of Complainant

Name of person to be questioned (the respondent)	To:
Address	Of:
Name of complainant	1.
Address	Of:

Consider that you may have discriminated against me contrary to the Disability Discrimination Act 1995 ("the Act") by unjustifiably

a) For a reason relating to my disability, treating me less favourably than you treat or would treat people to whom that reason does not or would not apply; or

b) Failing to take steps which it was reasonable in all the circumstances to have to take to prevent your employment arrangements or premises putting me at a substantial disadvantage compared with people who are not disabled.

Give details including a factual description of the treatment received or the failure complained of. Describe any relevant circumstances leading up to this and include any relevant dates or approximate dates.	2.
* Complete if you wish to give reasons, otherwise delete	3. I consider this treatment or failure on your part may have been unlawful because*
	4. Do you agree that the statement in paragraph 2 above is an accurate description of what happened? If not in what respect do you disagree or what is your version of what happened?
	5. Do you accept that your treatment of me or any failure complained of was unlawful? If not
	a) Why not?
	b) Do you consider your treatment of me or your failure to take action was justified for any material or substantial reason(s)?
Any other questions you wish to ask	6.
* Delete as appropriate. If you delete the first alternative, insert the address to which you want the reply to be sent.	7. My address for any reply you may wish to give to the questions raised above is * that set out in paragraph 1 above/the following address

Signature of Complainant ....

Dated ....

N.B. By virtue of section 56(3) of the Act, this questionnaire and any reply are (subject to the provisions of section 56 and any orders made under that section) admissible in proceedings under Part II of the Act and a Tribunal may draw any inference it considers is just and equitable from a failure without reasonable excuse to reply within a reasonable period, or from an evasive or equivocal reply, including any inference that the respondent has discriminated unlawfully under Part II of the Act.

The Disability Discrimination Act 1995 Section 5(1) and 5(2)

Response to Questionnaire

Note: Before completing this reply form, we advise you to prepare what you want to say on a separate piece of paper. If you have insufficient room on the reply form for what you want to say, continue on an additional piece of paper, which should be attached to the reply form and sent to the Complainant.

Enter the name of the person you are reply to (the Complainant).	To:
Enter the Complainant's address.	Of:
Enter your name (you are the Respondent).	1.
Enter your address.	Of:
Complete as necessary.	Hereby acknowledge receipt of the questionnaire signed by you and dated: which was serviced on me on
If you **agree** that the statement in paragraph 2 of the questionnaire is accurate, delete the second sentence. If you **disagree**, delete the first sentence and complete the second. (See paragraphs 23–24 for guidance)	2. I agree that the statement in 2 of the questionnaire is an accurate description of what happened. I disagree that the statement in 2 of the questionnaire in that:

* Delete as appropriate (see paragraphs 25–28 of the guidance).

3. I *accept/*dispute that my treatment of you or any failure to take action on my part was unlawful.

Include any reasons which in your view explain your treatment of the applicant or any decision not to take action.

*My reasons for disputing this are

Include any reasons which in your view justify your treatment of the applicant or any decision not to take action.

*I consider my treatment of you or my failure to take action justified for the following material and substantial reason(s).

Replies to questions in paragraph 6 of the questionnaire (see paragraph 29 of the guidance).

4.

Delete the whole of this sentence if you have answered all the questions asked in the questionnaire. If you have not answered all the questions delete as appropriate and give your reasons for not answering.

5. I have deleted (in whole or in part) the paragraph(s) numbered ...... above, since I am **unable/unwilling** to reply to the relevant questions in the correspondingly numbered paragraph(s) for the following reasons.

Signature of respondent...
Date ....

(see paragraph 30 of the guidance)

How to serve the reply form on the Complainant

- If you wish to reply to the questionnaire we strongly advise that you do so without delay.
- You should retain and keep in a safe place the questionnaire sent to you and a copy of your reply.
- You can serve the reply either by delivering it in person to the Complainant or by sending it by post.
- If you send it by post, we advise you to use the recorded delivery service (*this will provide you with evidence of delivery*).
- You should send the reply form to the address indicated in paragraph 7 of the Complainant's questionnaire.

INDEX